*"WHEN YOU'RE HAPPY
YOU GOT WINGS ON YOUR BACK
REPOSEZ VOS OREILLES à GOA;
WE'RE ONLY ONE KISS AWAY"*

Sunny Jetsun

*"You are a little Planet * A Jewel in the Sky"*

"When You're Happy You Got Wings On Your Back ~ Reposez Vos Oreilles à Goa; We're Only One Kiss Away"

Sunny Jetsun

Books by the Same Author:

Driving My Scooter through the Asteroid Field
Coming Down Over Venus ~ "Hallo Baba"
'Light love Angels from Heaven.
New Generation, Inspiration, Revolution, Revelation.
All the Colours of Cosmic Rainbows'
*'Green Eve * Don't lose the Light Vortex **
My brain's gone on holiday ~ free flowing feelings'
'Surfing or Suffering ~ together * Sense Consciousness
fields of a body with streams and stars of hearts'
'Psychic Psychedelic'
'Streaming Lemon Topaz Sunbeams'
*'Invasion of Beauty *FLASH* The Love Mudras'*
'Patchouli Showers ~ Tantric Temples'
'It's Just a Story ~ We Are All The Sun, Sweet Surrender'
Anthology #1 ~ 'Enjoy The Revolution'
Anthology # 2 ~ 'Love & Freedom ~ Welcome'
'He Lives In a Parallel Universe'
'Queen of Space ~ King of Flower Power ~ dripping Rainbows'
'All Love Frequency ~ In Zero Space'
*Peace Goddess*Spirit of the Field*The Intimacy Sutras*
'Heavenly Bodies ~ Celestial Alignments
Feeling ~ Energy that Is LOVE in Itself'
'I've been to Venus & back*These Are Real Feelings*
Let the Universe Guide Your Heart*through Space'
The Kiss in Slaughterhouse 6

Books by the Same Author:

Originally Published as Ciel Rose

'Sadhu Sadhu Sadhu ~ "All Beings Be Happy" ~ Shanti, Shanti'

'Trilogy of Vibrations ~ The Oneness of Life'

'Each Fragment of Life Is Sacred ~ These Are Your Children'

'Young Women Spin On Their Doorsteps At Dusk'

'Life Is Simple, Sharing ~ Loving Kindness from the Heart'

'The Universe Coming Across the River'

*

Originally Published as Sunny Revareva

'Pure Light ~ Cosmic * Sweet Heart ~ We've All Got Stars Inside'

'Perfect Love ~ No Mind * Star Light ~ Come Alive'

'True Freedom ~ Natural Spiritual Beauty ~
Here * Now ~ Gems of Eternity'

*

This book is arranged from 'Surreal' notes made from Inspirational
conversations with friends during the 2007/08 winter season
in Anjuna, Goa * "Thank you all" ~ Om Shanti, Shanti *** ☺

*

It's the Universe

We are the Moon * we are the Arctic ~ seabed
We are Green land too brother. You are the hurricane
on the streets of Houston, we are COSMIC.
Don't let anyone tell you that ~
"You are not from the Quantum, Crystal Space Ship!"
"You are a little Planet * A Jewel in the Sky"
"Welcome Aboard * Welcome to Earth"

*Free Cosmic * Global Id*
*Our Number *You are a Star coming from the Stars**
When it's Perfect it's Perfect. "Please don't spike me!"
"I'll have some of that juice and call you when I get lost....
4.30 am. wake-up call for migrant workers; Indian Temple bells ring!
Puja ~ why do we believe in anything, Rama, Karma, Dhamma?
And Why believe all the crazy stuff that marches us to Wars?
'Live and Let Live' ~ Isn't that your password, holy mantra?
Krishna's Absolutely not going to change his divine Mind.
Caste will be existing in years to come; try a New deal!
*"I feel brighter every day" * "This Paradise is too quiet"*

*

GALAXY GRAFFITI
A lot of contrast, underground, sub-conscious,
realisation, being, nature, spirit, free streaming ~
Open to the random Cosmos, synchronicity, here now.
Everywhere you learn a sublime language of Creation.
What do you want to express?
The right balance of light & dark, chiaroscuro intimacy.
Atoms of Infinite Relativity

*

Banking Cartel's ~ Easing It Qualitatively
Manifesto: To Nationalise Banks, where did all our money go?
What did I get out of it? Nothing! Everything is a Ponzi fraud!
Public relations, advertising, elections full brainwashing scams.
Enhanced interrogation Techniques whilst they're Torturing you!
Only your beliefs keep you going, that's your strength!
'Secular Terrorism' we pay for the Peace not the house.
Only humans can see the rainbows I didn't know that.

*

Observing

Discipline that Mind.
Meditation is Silence.
Easier to skin-up ~
Beauty of the herb.
"Seen people panicking going to a Yoga class!"
Promises me Peace.
Controlling your Mind by witnessing it, seeing the path.
Don't want to live by 'Expectations' - 'Rules' but...

*

Turmeric Lollipops

Where we come in, looking at the birds, the bees.
Whatever comes up, you can't do anything for it
Only being it ~ In that State everyone has their own realities.
Whole picture's turning around ~ Upside down karma...
Stand on your head, look from the other side, perception!
We are lost in Space inside a galaxy * but we don't know it.
Super Illusions of Permanence ~ what is more Impermanent?
Sudden death, Reality check, people can go as quick as dodos.
Allowance ~ "this is it".... statistically this is Scientifically Proven,
trying to fathom the Unfathomable! Goes further up & Closer in
that's why people go on psychedelic trips to lose their identity,
entering into another elliptical dimension * A New World Star.
How is the Observer? Connected through the feelings ~
The Mind is receiving & transmitting until the last breath.
Separating oneself from that the 'I', 'Me' 'Mine not thine!'
Going out of it ~ Zeroing on Something else.
It's not me ~ It's not my Mind only its FORM.
In SPACE who Knows (Mind); what else is there?
Everything is so commercial nothing more is true.
Hey shut up Mr. Shark, Mrs. Piranha & Queen Maya.
"The Observer of the Mind is Me, I am not the Mind"
'I am Perfect Space as Reality'

<u>Beautiful tree</u>
"Didn't you throw water over the helmet?"
"I know it's the Mouth of the River ~
'The Swillers' rampaging In the Season of Shanti.
Logical Norman hanging marigold garlands around her neck.
"I can put up with the Bullshit when it's 36° and I'm high!"
Putting on my psychedelic turban and it's All Celestial
Seeing Stars in the Astral Heavens or from Google Earth?
"So what are we supposed to do?" ~ "Reflect the best for All"
Drop Anchor gorgeous
*

<u>Happy Quantum You</u>
Breathing through a Mask ~
Lying High in an Oxygen tent.
Medication, Meditation on Prana being there.
Treasures of Love * Non-existence by itself.
"No fear of death for those Protected by the dhamma ~
Everything is combined together holistically ~ Nothing Is
Definitely a Unity/Id/entity * n/either the Sun or Moon.
It's all an Illusion of the faculties of our fallible senses.
Permanency is only a Concept in Cosmic Atomic fields"
"No soul just Mind's reaction to Objects in infinite Space"
*

<u>Twisted, Resistant Stereo-Types * No Reality</u>
Anybody with balloons wrapped around his head is on drugs!
Now Illegal to send them into space, they burst, fall into the sea,
the fish eat them and die; like our holy cows eating plastic bags.
She's from one of the nicest shanties, which way to Babylon?
Unreal Paradise made into a brainwashed Nightmare!
'LIMITED MIND IS A LIMITATION of SPACE'
Good Karma only exists as a concept.
"You are everything to my ego dear"

666 in Zionism is?

Out of thought; 'Stop Thinking About It' if You can!
Changing flames in space, looking at the Unformed.
Listen to spiraling galaxies to Silent boundlessness.
Total Infinite Peace ~
Allowing the No Thoughts in No Space.
"How deep, boundless do You wanna go?"
Deeper, deeper of course ~ until a moment's pure harmony.
'That Thinking, Repetitive Thing', the old record spinning round.
Need to use that Instant ~ right thing comes in at the right time.
Choosing to think when you need to think or reflecting in silence.
Always Omnipresent Space ~ existent in fields of dark matter.
Whole thing, you are this unique moment; always being as it is.
Breathing in an energetic Lotus; a Timeless multi * Dimension.
Enjoying the colours of cherry blossoms, receptive to nature.
Reaction of the thought processes * "I'm Super Sensitive"
"Hitting me like a Ton of Bricks!"
*

Natural beauty of Love

Watching the Mud (mind) hole bubbling.
"I understand E*motion, I am Emotional!"
Mind has been Conditioned for 100000000's of years!
Want to go back to the Natural State ~ "Welcome to Earth"
Wise man purring with a green eyed Persian pussy on his lap.
"Let go of it"
Switch\:/to Feeling.
Stay Inside your body
Universal Rhythm playing.
Align Your Brain with it ~ Universal energy.
"You Are the Stars" * nevertheless still True.
Who can complain ~ when it's sunny every day?
It's the mother who makes life ~ things come to be.
We Worship the Spirit * female elementals.
Cosmic dancing all about Creation being

Within the moment
Realisation In the Rainbow ~
Making a biochemical Mandala
Sacred Geometry
Mudras opening up the circuits
In your electromagnetic field.
Psychiatrists have the highest rates of suicide,
they become 'Mental' Off their rockers, themselves.
Attached to problems
Then there's the Dentists dead in the surgery.
And Italians burning candles for your soul
*
Rainbow Merkaba
Fluorescent krill crawling on the glass ceiling ~
Making a wave engulfed in the Openness of a face.
Yantra tattoos spreading across her full, erect nipples!
Abstract expressionism in tune with a smiley Moon ☺
With energy frequency ~ Consciousness
The Present over a kaleidoscopic bridge ~
Receiving Intuition/ by their own way
*Transition * letting go of the past*
The New is a bright Crystal way
'Not The Knowledge'
Knowledge is for everyone different.
Knowing boxes, knowing clear rivers
The Space In between is 90% what we go on.
Holistic bridges from all sides
High energy essence healing
Mind's filling in content between the Spaces.
Intellect Internet enter net Inner net ethereal net ~
Surrendering to Kama's & Rati's flexible, seductive charms.
Defining writhing buttocks by building Frames of Reference.
One phone call ~ just make the connection!

Radharani
We looked her up
Just happening ~ fully loved groove
Amazing expressions under her wet glistening lashes

*

Sufi Dancing
'The 5 Tibetan exercises'
Spinning turning focusing ~ on the Point
Singing to God on the full power of green sprouts.
Keep on going, healing a disease is a big teacher.
Sick from Thinking, try realizing Discernment.
This energy finds you ~ it's not a theory

*

Seeing Dangers Projecting
They stopped believing in God!
Fell off a Spaceship
"We'll cross that bridge when we come to it"
Even if you don't get robbed
*You Rob Your*self, needing Protecting!*
A whirling Quantum Sufi Impregnating us ~
We could be, are, whoever we wanted to be.
Take the disease suit off (MS) Open up the cells.
Gave away your own Responsibility ~ to the Doctor!
Interpol ~ Running it through at 10,000 faces per sec.
Drugs paranoia, sad for our sacred Spirit
Depression putting me into a lunch box.
Will I be sleeping forever on your couch?
Goa Therapy, natural, psychedelic vibe
*Spaced Out * Spacing In*
with your out of balance feelings.
Withdrawing myself ~ Cutting Off
A view, depression of the emotions.
Making changes ~ in reflective chemistry
Another Mystical Mystery

Danced Out!
Now Scientists are starting to change their tune
'Energy leaps' ~ Attention span.
As soon as it starts it happens ~
*It's only You who gives it **Form***
Focus your Intention ~ sensational changing Space.
"Bring me the most beautiful woman in the World!"
Devotion with a spiritual heart of consciousness.
Such Big waves ~ Times come around again
Rely on something in Yourself Not on TV. AI.
Try a natural, smoothie Yoni Massage

*

Blackmailed by the Son of a Crown Prince;('Independent' 16/2/2008)
"Prince Bandar Head of Saudi National Security and the one being
investigated for allegedly taking over 2 Billion pounds in bribes
from BAE flew to London on December. 6th 2007 to 'Lobby' for.....
7/12/07 Blair wrote to the Attorney General and Serious Fraud Office.
'Call it off the Saudis are threatening GB. with more Terrorism!'
Another 7/7; Loss of British lives on British streets!"
They'll hold back their Info. on Terrorists & Suicide Bombers!
On their way from Mecca with Dirty Bomb fully laden belts.
And we fell for it of course, what a dirty trade of Politics!

*

'Has a Reputation as a Hell Raiser' ('The Independent' 22/7/2008)
'Radovan Karadzic the man accused of Masterminding the Srebrenica
massacre has finally been arrested in Serbia. His co-indictee General
Rathko Mladic who is accused of the massacre of 7500 Muslim men
and boys in the 'safe haven' of Srebrenica was also indicted
for the Siege of Sarajevo (10,000 dead), is still on the loose!
The worst atrocity in Europe since the end of 2nd World War'
'Many bodies broken by mechanical diggers.....
yet the town remains ethnically cleansed'

<u>Conjuring an Alien</u>
Top Secret Spirits
Keeping the Mind Open ~
To be able to witness the Mind,
detached, compassionate Mind.
'You saw what you saw, You believe what you believe'
Being here now ~ going through the Sound Barrier
to Infinite space ~ there is no end

*

<u>Music on the Hauptstrasse</u>
Can't call it Psy*Trance
don't know what to do ~
She's gone into a deep Depression!
And I got a Ticket just for doing a Headstand.
"You are such an amazingly, delicate flower"

*

<u>Language * Happening</u>
In Goa every day's a holiday Baba.
Speaking only Love words
And you will be cured.
Makes sense if you find yourself
In a shining, crystal hologram expression.
Don't hold yourself in fields of other reflection
Open your 3rd eye to look from Inside ~
At your Playground....
Not limited by a 'Belief System'
Morphing, Shape-Shifting your Sun
You Are Not ~
Cosmically Divine Is
Perfection Is continuously changing
Sparkle Out >*< from Yourself
Lightning Up themselves ~
The Now Is I

Cynical Website

You're bound to get mugged in a 'black out'
How to designajetengine.com, howtodofuckall.com
˙ because fuck it all is what it's about! Is it mind?
Without trying we're all creative ~
Existence In Us whether we like it or Not bro.
All this Freedom; how much Backshish Rules?
We live in our own bubble or a blob!
So bloody Repressive & corrupt.
Where's the Amazing Natural Balancing?
Getting their Income from drugs, illegal everything ~
In a Medieval country selling itself as a Modern Power
to do what? Take another bribe; violence, ignorance,
& everybody shuts up and is quiet, guilty and afraid.
Fascinating Interface with a Top Mafia Brain.
Don't Blame it on the organic watermelons

*

Golden Native Skin

They were aliens from Andromeda's Tranquility base.
'Immortals' not Untouchables ~ it's all spirally * spiritual.
Only way to reach Krishna, nice and lush not in a rush.
'He doesn't beat about the bush', 180,000 lovely wives.
"Luckily I was too innocent to pick it up!" Authoritatively.
'The Proper Propaganda Brainwashing Program'
"Repeat after me" - "Do as I say don't do as I do."
Schools of demons in bloody wolves' clothing…
Threw the baby over the hill ~
over the horizon, A. I. Cloning.
He's in Psy*trance, tuning in to other surreal realms.
What is happening, finally freaking out in realisation.
Sailing through Portals of the hypothalamus & heart.
Down the river we go ~

Infinite Infant

I think he had a Peruvian wife, sold the company, moved down there.
As a child I asked the Rabbi if he'd read the Sumerian 'Twelfth Planet'.
Realising the importance of reality's 3d effect ~
"Is there a lightning flash when that starts to happen?"
In sub-conscious Space going through the shimmering veil.

*

Knit one Pearl one

Getting what I want one day, miss the next.
"She needed to be taken out the game and
put in the hospital down the road", he said.
If you know the way in ~ entry to the Jungle,
experience being in the most beautiful groves.
"People will believe what they want to believe"
"I'm sure I'll go through the darkest loop"
I'll get it in the neck of time ~
Being refreshed & replenished

*

Organic Polarity Smiling

Somebody said, the Heart, I don't know if it's true or not,
'has more neurons than the mind'.
Imagine the duality ~ Feeling Chaos, mass confusion.
You could have nightmares about it but it's all synergy.
It's a very quiet place, the seat of Understanding.
I've gone off duality changed to impermanent relativity ~
It's only how people interpret signals that makes matter.
Going back in the mind, insecurity, fear, loss, grief and ego.
In reality ~ where are we gettin' that 'actual reality' from?
Its duality(:)bright & dark with chiaroscuro's dancing light.
There's definitely a hidden hand, it's not what you think.
'There is nothing new under the Sun'

Your Aura
Buddha's Mirror
The Sun shines ~
The Solar System is him
What else is there?
Shooting Ayur*Vedic ultra*violet flames
*

Foreign Sputniks
Rays from the Stars ~
Reptile Race from Mars?
'Naked English lessons
for Russian Tongues'
*

Bonded to Mahalakshmi
"They say when a baby's in the Womb it gets the smell
of its Mother which it will always remember, all of its life."
"They arrested me because I had no shoes on in Germany"
Everything there on TV. has to be sanctioned by America.
"No one likes it, everyone puts up with it!"
*

You're just a worker you do what you're told!
Addicted to smart Technology you hold in your hand.
In the future we'll all be living in AI. synthetic clouds.
Programmed & conditioned by nano*bots working
for a Holy Dictatorship of the High-Tech grid.
Disconnecting you from your eternal-being.
The relentless exploitation & destruction
of Pachamama by corporate sociopaths!
Making new enslaved, sub-human chips.
You have been implanted * now You're
numbers in an Internet Matrix process.
Welcome to Terra as a Virtual App.
Automatons, no critical thinking,
remote, no reasoning or feeling!

Tata Condition

How to Govern a Kingdom?
Making It happen ~ Potentiality
Big limits to what people can do.
Walkin' skeletons and human reality!
Learning about human Identity, human dignity.
Let's have the Fun part not the manifested problems.
All trying to figure out who we are in this world brother!
Bigger potential than beggar potential if you're spiritual!
"Life is an Opportunity"
'Your truth is not my reality'

*

Keep an Open Mind

Not true from your point of view. "Ole!"
Expectations and dramas even constant denials.
Who Am I? One to discover ~ an enlightened Processing!
Keep them all in the herd ~ brainwashed NanoRobot snout.
Nothing to Live for ~ Clockin in, clockin off, for fuckin' nout!
Amazing how they keep them all going to the factory gates.
Feels normal at her Aspergic group in Emergency Ward 10.
Feeling dancing freely with wild red hot Carmen on the table
because People would think we were Crazy!
A Mad, sexy witch embraced my Uniqueness.
Cosmological Not what you are Identifying with.
Never forget to ~ Simply remember to remember.
Branded Brain dead, dry cleaned, pressed, starched & Ironed.
The Black Pope, Darth Vader Knights living over the Holy See.

*

Another Interpretation

Gotta let the light Shine * Unprogrammed Programming.
Worshipping, Celebrating in Nature, Spirit, truth & Love.
Cultivating the herbs, don't get stoned on thistles, bud.
How you gonna squirm out of the Lake of fire?
On DNA wavelets ~

12

Om Mani Padma Hum
'Inside the Ocean of the Heart'.
Soft landing on Uranus, climbing Mons Veneris
Inside a hot and wet Love Relationship
It's fighting with your sociopathic Mars.
It's listening to your deeper Venus
It's feeling your Atomic Sun.
Ultra sensitive to Osmosis
*

Traveling in the Mind
'A Rough Guide to the Quantum World'
Not Planet Hollywood or Silicon tits Valley!
Not Palaces of Illusion or bodies of delusion
It's boundless, beyond Universes' of the Mind.
'One Giant Leaping', thru purple spiral galaxies.
Why Insist? Powerless to resist or desist ~
until the last drop, thought, in the Conscious.
Travelling with your Supra Spirit
In your full humanity
*

Carbon-Offsets Gimmicks - What did ya say Shelia?
A Virtual money market based on Pollution still developing.
You can buy your way out of it, pay someone for their share!
How many lights are in a Palace, Guvnor? Richer Consumer!
A plastic coated Australia floating in Pacific Oceanic currents.
"The World wouldn't be the same without rats!"
Original Organic nursery, a Green, Holistic Hotel & Ashram
Offerings of barley & Ghee; Consciously letting go of a body.
"It's our destiny to die" & have an energetic rebirth,
the light is always shining above the Quantum tree!
Invoking waves of higher frequency ~
Coming into the Reality of your Mind.
Images are your own creation; projections & recognition.
Liberation's Interpretation Simultaneously

Sat Guru

Not Lazy ~ looking for a Yogananda to believe in.
When there is Resonance there's a Swarmi
Only natural laws
Simplicity easy to accept
Working in harmonies ~ less tumult.
Immediate transmission of Information
She asked me to grow wild flowers on her grave.
"You are You giving yourself Consequences"
She didn't Mind
Free will
*

Quicksilver Hermes

The Messenger guiding Souls to the Divine.
Through you is Reflected ~ 'The gift of God'
You make a stand.
Rainbow of benediction
Responding to the call
Allowing an angel to caress your heart.
We have it All in us
*

Starting at 0

Murmuring ***34 + 21 Energetic fields***
Full Power Tree Goddesses stirring in the breeze
"I'm born in this body" ~ Life Forces Processing...
"Elle flip quoi!"
"First there's nothing then there is you
~ then there's a problem"
"Just give yourself the Best my friend"
'Male mind, electric, Anti-Clockwise
Female emotion, magnetic, Clockwise'
On a grid of Christ Consciousness
Infinite spirals of a golden mean
No beginning ~ no ending

Magid*ich
Throwing the picture, like old runes on the ground
Seeing how it is, you know before it happens
Pre*sense in the Present ~ Living the gift of Life force
Allowing yourself to flower as a child of God
"In to it"

*

Symbolic death
'To die or not to die' ~ that is not the answer!
Make your own Cross, let the Captain beware.
Graffiti flash hash, can't I go away feeling better?
Full Freedom; Heaven help it, the writings on the wall.
Not conditioned, full No-Mind * Supra*surreal Paintings.
"Bring it on" "Show me the Power" "What you got!?"
Full Crazy, Full blood, I'm in Space as a flower ~
'Can't come ~ Ephemera on Earth.
Skied across white Russia with a damask ideogram.
Sailed a Dory to Portugal with a stranger stranger.
"Everyone's a teacher not all with the right answers"

*

Cosmic Alpha Baba & LA Siren
"Brought a gram of Charlie as a courtesy" "do you want
to go to a Party with White Coke whores up in the hills?"
Healing, this is happening right now ~ ubiquitous attention.
Hitting the flow ~ coming back to the 4th dimension
Just allowance to go through the In-between Space.
Meditative driving into a multiple entry artificial crater.
Accepted, "If you don't feel it you may never have it"
Selling them Everything they didn't need!
She was making diamond water, brainwashed, conformed.
"No problems only solutions, no questions only answers"
"I couldn't make it up, I'm not that clever!"
"Do you live on a toxic planet? We'll not come for a visit then"
Allowance as existence runs through you ~ flame same same!

<u>Inner Revolutionary's Red Tulips</u>
Freedom of Speech, free will, yes or no? Your Moon...
has to be full or we're only parrots, don't know anything.
The Universe is Existing throughout You ~
Oil her and chase her; Party on, in No-Mind!
Revelation it's a moment ~ with a full magnetic totty machine.
Out ~ straight through the heart to the Cosmic channel
You can't go backwards, have to Allow unfolding, change ~
Don't want to manifest a Russell's Viper, pitter patter of a crow.
Drops, bombs of MDMA, Not Napalm clusters or Daisy busters!
*
<u>Let her bake cakes!</u>
Winding up the Mind; Double Aries, Pussies' Pure Ring.
On the Planet; Remote Sensing, just behind the clouds.
Time is an Illusion ~ "Somehow I missed the shuttle flight"
Did you ever try stepping outside, beyond the Mind concept?
Relaxing with everyone at Shiva Palace, see you in Kiev.
A dynamite dancer with the Prison keys, flying out
with a magic case to Düsseldorf, my mission to do....
Wonder over Wonder over Wonder over Wonderful ~
No No No; Yes Yes Yes. "Happens when it should happen"
Can get more than their experience, needs just a candle.
They know you're not going to give them a line of Coke!
A little bit wobbly energy ~ she's a smoker for sure.
19, perfect, juicy peaches, you would like to eat her.
5 plugs aligned to intimate relations, follow the lines.
This is all an Illusion, at the final stage door.
Peace incarnate and protection of a Spirit
Cosmic Joke, 'we take it all too seriously!'
Gratitude is opening the heart ~ you have to be excellent
or you don't make it; people will project onto you at once.
There's a crisis everywhere ~ infertility from Mother Corn.
'Gentec' has the Patent, distracted by default programs.
Sometimes I forget to feel

*Not in 3D * Back to Eden*
Cleaned the lake with a sacred Mantra
Putting the energy in ~ to what you crave
Food, water, air, whacked out on sugar!
Consciousness is Alive, needs to be fed.
Avoiding Predators, Piranhas, Sharks in Armani.
Energy is money, bedazzling, cash registering.
It's bloody common sense but nobody's got any.
Remember the Program and you'll do fine!
Be Safe get Insurance; what are they learning?
#1 Military Technology, defense spending
before you'd buy a seed!
*

Sun Compass
Hitch hiking to Sin with the Vice Squad
The Eagle, National bird of America ~
Yeah, until they DDT'd them all DEAD!
Killed off the Brown Bear, symbol of California.
Let's do it, we're two adults from Venus, Yeah!
It's their own experience ~ if you have to be sick
you'll be sick awhile then go through to Paradise.
Trust is totally different energy
*

*Trans Somatic * Vegan Gelati*
Cannabis Ice Cream at the rampant, 'Wet Dream Restaurant'
*Organic Mescaline cake, nothing to do * Cosmic experience.*
Full of lights in your pupil. 'It's all Funtastic, sweetest smiles ~
Creating by allowing it to happen, getting up out of the grave!
'You can't be loving if you're not free ~ not free if not loving'
She was completely in the light, delicious ephemeral sprite.
She looked so different, Alive not nervous, without stress.
Keeps me going, no fear jumping into a cream rainbow.
'Thought is ultimately expressed by L'amour'
"This is Not a Dream Sunshine"

<u>The much higher vibe of two suns celebrating</u>
*"Dark & light are the same * same ~ but different shades.*
No mass hypnosis or guilt trips, nothing to do but Enjoy.
You can choose the experience you want to live.
Yoga discipline, opposite to the Tantra shortcut"
Puja, calling the Spirit in the right atmosphere
for the muse to come ~ the Channel is One.
Words come by themselves.
The Greatest Pleasure ~
Everything can be Meditation
'Dreaming Yoga' is the nicest,
for me making the whole circle.
Mass-Illusion is in Fashion!
Pushing the Pendulum to balance
You can Bless it
*

<u>Reality's Duality</u>
"My grief is for Myself"
Now I see the Why, otherwise it wouldn't have happened.
A Nice story, a full film, another ego trap.
Name it, tell her, "your husband is dead"
Own It; a new Step, a new trip ~
"Why did you Allow Yourself to go without me?"
Shocking but making it clear
That it's now like this......
Things happen in all sorts of ways.
Hard to let you go
"Is this Paradise?"
*

<u>It just is what it is</u>
"I just walked in to see what condition my condition was in"
"It's a jungle outside the Zoo!"
"It's a Zoo outside the jungle!"

Attraction of Red Ganesh

Worse than a hyper-Megalomaniac, 'It's bad decisions!'
All the people were brainwashed, by the media, their job.
Saved by Darjeeling chili hotter than a Mexican tamale.
We become ill when we're out of balance
Go sit on a flat roof
Go sit in a dome
Energies go around ~
Enchantment to enchantment.
"I know best"
Put the front door at the north
and keep some water by it for riches.
Putting Ganesh in the North East; his direction
by the door facing inside removing any obstacles.
Black Ganesh pointing south to destroy all the enemies.
Inside out ~ sacred Tantric secrets
"It's real, it works, it's dangerous"
Lakshmi goddess of wealth out riding her owl

*

Fertile Celts * Ancient Soul

Listen to the music & love the mystery not misery!
They made it easy for the Modern man.
Turning up at the Temple in a three-piece suit.
We're here in the now ~ has to be what's in the now
Let it manifest what it wants to be ~
And you hold the light, hold on tight!
Knee-jerk reaction ~ which is the Mind, gets involved.
"Listen mate!"
"I know where I'll be, can't speak for anyone else"
"Here's comin' the Green * clairvoyant Queen!"
"Drugs they scare me, It lowers me"
Could be stressful, could be fun
In the Temple of Love

19

Patchouli * Flower
Offering of garlands to Lakshmi,
Kali Musk, Shiva Sandalwood.
Everything is Krishna's ~ Lila divine playboy, Cosmic Baba.
Kali makes Shiva a God dancing on his chest.
Rather have him like that than brainwashed sour & grumpy
Put it out there ~ are there any others waiting for it?
It's living with them whatever energy you send out,
spins around the Earth ~ getting it back from the Universe.
'Satyagraha' Non-violence won India a sort of Independence.
Still like that, clobbering them, changed their lathi for a Taser!
'Ahimsa' ~ "No one will come out of a Nuclear War Alive ~
*

The Weather of Jungle Law
Kill & survive, DNA. man is an Aggressive, a Territorial Animal.
Would you become Sri Caligulaji in India or a converted Asoka?
Smouldering in a teepee, candle on a skull, Incense burning.
"Anything that robs the world of joy is the Devil"
'Keep an Open Mind on that one' ~ All for the same 'Divine'.
His Karma was blown up by a soon to be extinct Tamil Tiger.
Hindu way ~ Shanti, tolerant you have to respect Forms.
Provoking a 'Holy War', tearing a mantra shawl for a safi!
Formlessness ~
*

Reflections of Inside * Outside
Shiva makes Mother nature feel like a woman.
Not easy to see him and stay alive.
Lights in the deepest jungle ~
You'll wake up to who you are.
The Interior of a Cosmic Mind
Maya free diving in Space ~
Space incorporates Mind * all yours.
Transcending it ~ through the heart
the part of man connecting with woman.

*Putting It Together * Beyond Mind*
It was Massive like a Mother*Spaceship ~
The Spaceship that never lands, "beam me in."
Woke me from my sleep, couldn't get over it.
Calm down take some Painkillers, No expectations!
"What the fuck's goin' on here then?"
Spontaneous no taboos, Open house....
We made it a Love House, pulling things in by their dicks!
Rampant Pussy Power ~ You know what thought can do?
Plastic up to the hilt, a big rabbit in a small winking hole.
This is not as satisfying as a natural woman.
*
*

Sizzling
No breeze
Lost in the 9 Bar
Off it floated ~
Pulled the plug
going straight thru it ~ filled up so full of shit.
We had to come here to see the Mountain
*
*

Captain of the trip
Independent journey traveling through the Mind ~
'Silence is Golden' Sex Surfing taking it to a peak.
Cut throat business the demand for purified virgins,
clearly outstrips supply ~ back to the roots level!
*
*

Commander Paranoia
Stargate's Open ~ Always in Time with the now
Monkey Mind Projects into the imaginary future.
I have many hearts, some girls have Big hearts.
Her mum was a burlesque girl, full doe eyes ~
*Her whole being * Is exceptionally beautiful.*
They've given us all those taboos to stop us enjoying ourselves.
Fraternising with your dearest enemy, sucking my juicy plums.

Found Paradise

Captured by one of the girls for a soapy bath at the Panama Cafe.
There was something in his spirit that said, "I'll go for it"
'This was Fertile ground' ~ the music is still playing.
"I'd never heard a sound like it"
They put lightening cream on his face.
Making 2nd class citizens acceptable to a white audience.
'Straighten Up and Fly Right'
Coming back from a bad war!

*

Zanzibar Cafe

'Went right from there to Mexico'
"Let there be Love ~"
'Nature boy's a smash!'
"The greatest thing you'll ever learn,
is just to love and be loved in return"
'Everything he touched turned to gold'
'They suffered a great deal of harassment'
KKK. burnt a cross on the front lawn!
Now we're really in it, let the powers guide you.
The smallest ride on the biggest wave ~
Unconditional Love Supreme

*

Tropicana Havana

Acapella ~ it's a beautiful Love song...
"Perhaps, perhaps, perhaps, bien, perfecto"
Such a black skin he was almost blue, magical.
The first black artist on black and white television.
Singing love songs to your white wife, in your living room.
Capitalist Sponsors anointing the black out of a natural star.
Who's negotiating to get a black man in front of a white band?
Identity crisis invading the homes of white supremacists.
"Madison Avenue is afraid of the dark"
He filled her heart ~ with red roses.

Arriving Never too Late ~ Just in Time
Best Wishes for a Cosmic Revolution ~
What to do?
Smoke a joint and be happy....
Energetic world, 5th dimension, just the thought.
It's not how much, it's the frequency ~ the beauty.
A molecular emissions scanner of a Fortune Teller...
Reversing Inorganic to organic not 'Inheritance of Loss'
"May you be blessed with 10,000 sons (& smiling daughters)"
We don't see it anymore as it's so obvious! Blind ignorance.
Matrix the duality trip ~ giving yourself (a sense of) structure.
Blocking the Kundalini ~ Just live the multi * dimensionality
On a Higher feeling, Never break into a relationship.
That you are the reincarnation of DNA spiraling ~
Human beings not human doers.
Every crystal will go 'Bang!'
*

Neptune * Vastness
You got a better offer! Over the Love energy
we can take over any threat from the Matrix.
Headaches in inclement atmospheric pressure.
Shock of the realization - Manifested in the body.
Ripples in the brain ~ a Heart Attack happening,
Cardiac arrest, originated 9 months before!
Nuclear Medicine dept. in the dungeon of the hospital.
The Legalised Killing Machines, S2 flying Stealth Invasion!
Incandescent Toxic chemicals found in uncultured Pearls.
Poisoning people to make them better, easing their pain!
It gets worse; It's a belief system where you get sicker.
Allow the grief, the anger, the suffering to transmute
into the love vibe ~ getting tuned into your frequency
Following it ~ being it ~ the Spirit has done its job.
'It's not what you know it's in the beingness ~

Five letters a week

Winning the lottery with Crystal Power!
"It could be you but won't be you." Hooked on those games.
Seeping into UK. online Casinos, like bacon, eggs & toast!
Going for life energy ~ Building up, collecting the Prana.
A Visionland Circus shining in the Solar Plexus
Growing Chakra Power, visceral, in the guts ~
Shifting the courage over your heart
Fuelled Chi pushing it up to the golden spinning sphere.
You say, "that it is" <<:>> upholding the 4th dimension.

*

Migrating Pods

'Orca Killers in Poseidon's Marina, Pacific Eden'
It can be a long, solitary, unbelievable, painful road
on a journey of liberation * swimming to procreation ~
100,000 deaths in a Chinese Earthquake at Wenchuan,
100,000 died in a Burmese hurricane! Pulled out alive ~
Unbelievably-Disaster on a massive scale!
No help at all from the military dictatorship!
All happening in a split-second
How do you face up to this?
"I see the Sun now coming up in you"

*

Allowing Spiritual energy fields ~
Working with 'Predatory Whales'
Swimming to the next gateway
Wherever you want to go
One with it * Alignments, currents flow ~
Expressive, clear thoughts over a 3rd eye.
Understandable process, how you do it.
Knowing & Allowing, giving & receiving.
If they're in fear they'll make more Fear.
Many different Options Menu ~
'Select All'

That rosy glow

(Exotic*Erotic Ball) Enjoying feeling, being, reflexes of it.
Witness for them to be free, in nature by doing ~ being it.
US' Miss. Demon or ~ Protection of the 1st Amendment.
Fighting for her right to be naked, in the State of Nudity!
"The woman who wants to force me into marriage is.....
'Performance artists, free speech experts & contortionists.
Spiritual choice of freedom, Thesaurus'-'spiritual democracy'
Don't have to be in the human fetish, petting zoo to be bitten!
Living-out a torrid, desirous fantasy ~ ever playful, non-violently.
Why wouldn't you want Priti's pink candy on the tips of her lips?

*

Higher state of Tao Allowance

Unfolding out of the moment ~ going beyond beyond.
No more this or that dilemma determining her drama!
Over my heart ~ broken by a soul-mate, greedy and sly.
Dissolving it as best as I could because I didn't Lie.
Allowed myself, my ego, eating lots of Humble Pie.
Out of empathy be honest with your*self. Day's making You!
Helped me a lot, now in the Presence of the All Knowingness.
Turn the cameras around, people Conditioned on that Level!
Reflecting their Paranoia ~ Filming their hands free, trancing.
Building a multi*dimensional field of Sense*Consciousness.
Don't be Attached to any Product as an Accessory of you!
Your basic Creation giving it out ~ with Unconditional Love.
With it they have the free choice, making no more tyranny.
Falling out of the Ego ~ no more hanging on, Let it jump!
'The tree is not caring where the leaf falls'
A Bird not worrying about building its nest
knowing there's a nest there for them.
It's naturally Singing

*

This Weapon

'It's a Peace Maker!'

Neti Neti * Clear Space
Understanding ~ between the words
I Love it ~ All of the Allowance
To go out to change ~ to flow
Turning the Key in a Lock ~
Key is Spirit + (*) the Lock is minus -
Synchronicity ~ allowing them to fall in One.
Key experiences...
It can open a Lock.
She lost the key ~
gave her the key back.
I can only be with someone who is Free
Same frequency ~ (being in) harmony.
Direct connection to/through the heart
*

Don't need any more Certified French Nightmares!
How to live through that change in experience?
Last chance ~ for turnaround can be dangerous,
to lose yourself so simple, you throw the game.
I allow myself ~ to experience ~ the Higher frequency
Being open to this Invasion of beauty, focusing on her smile.
Fluffy Concentration, Control/Issues with the Yoga, discipline!
Focused Attention on the body level, has to love herself more.
"She had a good life with you" ~ isn't that what we aspire to?
Step back, 'Observe the mind' - essential eastern philosophy.
Acting it out in Zero space, they can hold it, going one side ~
or another. Right, Wrong, as long as it has some devotion.
It's up to you, You're a Creator & the Creator makes You.
"I do the best, expressing tenderly the things I Love"
Loving blondes especially Bottichelli's beauties full of ecstasy.
When it comes to eating a Perfect Peach in happy penetration.
As long as you're fully with it, no illusions in Your*Maya*self ~
38 kilos and ringing wet; about me being happy, in a groove.
Total Abundance at the feet of rainbow coloured Krishna

<u>You throw out your own Wave</u>
In 3 D.~ Switching the frequency
Inorganic to Organic 'EM's'...
5th dimensional elementals alive!
The Magician of your own beingness
Alchemical processing * higher, lighter frequencies ~
Trying to figure it out is no use, mind only knows **Forms**
Not Space * just have to experience it, it's coming out
Of my heart.
My best friend left today, Thank God.
A win, win, situation, seeing them when you want to.
Yes, Yes, Yes, Thank You; everyone gets to go home.
The body Consciousness will tell you.
I'm not the type for that.
"I'll put the button on the suit this way not that way"
With the Allowance ~ of the Trust you're building Up.
Your thought frequency in an Etheric body ~ Manifest & get it
*

<u>Progressive Circles Crushed</u>
Sensing Mother Russia's Infinity ~ in Prehistoric cave paintings....
A Grey witch healing with lemon budgerigars perched on her shoulder.
Entrancing magical myths, sprites and there's always enough....
Creating freedom, Vertical power structures need Cosmic links.
Slaves to a Mad man's dream ~ the Conditioning curse.
'We have to do Something to get Something'
Beingness not doingness ~ Performing the 7th Symphony.
'Separating their life and their 'every day' life!'
'Capitalist Pirates and the Dictatorship of the Proletariat'
How can you disregard the Siege of Leningrad comrade?
Changed his 12 gram. golden watch for horse fodder!
"Never Surrendered, never lost hope with Shostakovich"
Nearby mounds, remains of the first Viking Conquerors.
Eternal Flames are burning in the White Nights

Faster BPM

Psychoactives*man on a mission, hard to realise how simple!
'Wow, Kapow' something greater playing with the U magnets.
Nothing Special ~ Pure human understanding of the essence.
Programming the Playful, coming naturally, growing Inside ~
Should be Accelerating their Minds more ° focus
"We get taught that we're stupid in school,
children ask very Intelligent questions"
Very Social ~ teaches us to sit still, don't move-freeze!
Cool thing to do ~ seeing where Intuition lands.
"If only Baba, if only"
*

Turmeric Buddha

More Personal ~ You can eat it.
Looking in the Mystical Mirror,
Vibrates, radiates * room lit up!
Higher faeries started to dance
In the Mind ~ Loving everybody
Oasis not a bubble; I'm into Cosmic Spirit.
Who's Locked into the brain? Talk to it…
about manipulation, about being faithful.
No one's going to fuck with my Mind…
No one's going to let my Mind fuck with me.
Sitting under an apple tree
*

"You get a wife ~ you find a good thing." You mean Person?
Loving everything * Supernaturalism without Attachment.
Mr. Cool at 15, "Wow here's a piece of fresh meat,
once you put your ding dong in there!"
'Her beautiful pink rose'
"The Greatest Lie is the One Closest to the Truth"
This big deception ~ the rippling effects.
"You Are the Sun * Looking at the Sun"

Psy Pilot * I feel like you're a beggar but you're really a King!
Escaping the Matrix, most of us are taught bullshit from birth.
Recognising All into it Together, breaking out of Conditioning.
To have a garden not ashes, all prophets say the same thing.
This is what makes all the difference in nature ~
Everything else stays the same or so you think!
Ever met someone who never had an original thought?
Free radicals back with a Vengeance, raises my spirit ~
Doesn't happen at home; sucked into the brainwashing Television spin.
Global human entity, forget about Conglomerate, Political Power Identity!
Economy is such a sophisticated, simple thing should be used to benefit ~
All of Our Children

*

Shambala Key
Every chakra in you is a Sun centre
*Same * Same for Mother Earth*
This Projection game you have ~
How can you live in that Golden cage?
Taking back the energy of the Buddha field.
Love or Money, you've made the Separation.
It will unfold by itself ~ at the high Altar of Unity.
Holding a frequency And the Vatican facing judgment!
Sitting together under the Ganesh tree in a timely warp.
"Do you want to believe their processes put in your Mind?"
Everything's Telepathic ~ 'It's your will where you want to be'
The bird transmuting on Earth; what has to be done?
Archetypes of the nicest genome

*

Stardust Kids
Miss Doreen Virtueé's 'Harmonic Convergence' 17/8/1987.
"I've been in Spaceships" ~ swallowing liquid Sunshine.
*10 9 8 7 6 5 4 3 2 1 Zero * it's here, it's happening now ~*
The Earth Angels' glinting Portal, linking to Nature's Altar.
*Keep seeing the flora & fauna * faeries playing in her hair*

<u>Prana * Allowance</u>
"Lock him up!"
"You missed the Best, seeing her burnt,
her head exploded!" It's just a body mate.
"I feel what you feel ~
I feel You * You feel me"
"to see a burning is a fast track to Enlightenment"
Looking into the Celestial Mirror.
Limitless beingness ~ comes out of it, into the air.
The Realisation that you have this same energy.
When You're in Love you feel each other ~
Realisation ~ the acceptance to See or not to See
or See whatever you want to See ~
"At least hold a Position Consciously"
'Owning It' ~ Cosmic impermanence, always changing.
Filtering through 20,000 motives running in you now
To get the one

*

<u>Under ~ Currents</u>
Don't fall into the angry trap ~ of Guilt & SINS
All the Fears ~ Burning You Psychologically.
Manifesting clearly at one of the seven gates.
Bringing up the teaching, realizing it and getting it…
More Alert in the Trust ~ becoming One with the Vessel.
If we die we die ~ If we live we live.
"I am in Love with an amazing woman"
Ex-communicated and sent to the Hell fires! Thanks a lot!
But he'd already got it! "Don't want your THREAT anymore"
The Process of ~ watching your thoughts all the time.
They're good, who cares? No doubt….
Going back to essential Prana breath ~
Consciously witnessing your own death.
Abstract Magic ~ depends on you.
You put it or you don't put it

She was from Mars not Venus!
"I've never met a lower chakra
as beautiful as this(')wet Vulva"
We don't open * we just follow ~
A sexual healing is occurring now.
Intense, good to not get stuck in the density.
A huge white light * Crown chakra
Shoals of spiritual fish swimming ~
up & down ~ Inside you ~ it's your vibration.
Life energetically dancing on a rosy pink pudenda.
I used to be a mermaid loving rainbow porpoises ~
Now feeling spaceships beaming down rays of light.
*

Ibis Imprisoning a Cyclops
Orbiting notebooks of psychic paintings.
They've chosen the veil of separation ~
To be in the material West, coming East.
Isn't each Individual on Earth so Important?
My lava lamp is pervenche ~ Odyssey of a white star.
Your strong ancient wisdom in rays of love experience.
Evolution guiding life on Earth * shape-shifting into Angel fish
We weren't dense until Martian conscience arrived with fear.
Got denser, more fear incarnating in this human body
*

Martian genes, no feeling emotional body, purely logic.
Cloning > separately < reality to spirit
'Impossible to separate us if|as we are One'
Life Partners ~ here to experience creation.
Putting codes in our DNA*which vibrations are coming down?
Miracles happened on this beach, in her Space * Time vehicle.
Lunar eclipse * full moon winter equinox stepping into a vortex.
Must always ask permission > Too weird for words.
"You told us to remind you who you are"
An ethereal UFO shot out of my head!

Hologram Babe

Expanding the boundaries of man & woman in the Universe.
*The first drop of Psychedelica * never the same again!*
"DROP ACID NOT BOMBS!" ~ Who's the Genius then?
Who's sitting on top of a San Pedro (Mescaline) cactus?
Then started my dramatic life ~
Lot of trippy people come with magic mind.
Feedback: there's a lot of Peter Pans here.
* No comparing the energy *
It's Cosmic Crystal everywhere
*
Star Bar

Have to Plug In
Sex in a bottle on the Luna crater.
Psychic Poppers in a Cosmic Clit
Who's always bending the Rules?
*Old gone * now New*
Say 'Yes' to this moment ~
Clear in the infinite desert
*Relief * release ~ best Catalyser*
Open to the Celestial sky above
*
At the Meteorite Motel

Knowing the 99 names of Allah ~
Keeps one silent for himself and creation.
She couldn't fly back with a broken Merkaba
Brought her a new flying model from the 5th dimension.
The next gift gave us a master Key ~
to reveal what is behind the Gate
And make it free ~ In your hands.
*This 'Knowingness' * this Is....*
Transmuting us to the Highest & Best for All
Burning the Ego ask Archangel Mike ~
*Through Mother Nature * Pachamama*

I wish

It's only a matter of comparison, 'oh eye it's brilliant chuck!'
"It makes you wanna pack it up and go and live in Africa
with the monkeys" Checking if she's won a Premium Bond.
You have to live your own thing, we get pushed into it.
Just an explosion of energy * looking for a light switch.
More people waking up, for sure this is Goa until ~
A whole different Program, Surveillance ^ Control.
If you fight against this corruption you'll have trouble!
Can't hold onto our structure ~ changes changing
Hard to be free ~ most got lost in the 'Maya' calendar.
Ambient chill out, "I'm a trance head Baba Meditating"
Don't need an explanation, looking for something new.
Take the moment in the beauty that it is ~
We can still directly feel it, sitting in an old people's home,
clutching the remote controller as if your life depended on it!

*

'Mind Kampf'

Mother lode, what's the rush? A flaming, steaming bush!
Don't need to lose the body, vertically or horizontally.
They'll create their own transmutation frequency ~
Difficult to Know & not to know ~ sensible Alternatives.
Disappearing ~ from Chile; "Don't trust anyone honey!"
I was falling asleep, thank you for the message/memory.
"No I do trust nature" ~ discernment ~ of a Tango Deva
Being in the middle is being in the now ~ You understand
Multi*dimensional forces ~ being in your reflection instantly.
Mercury*Venus combining in beautiful spaces synchronically
All the micro-organisms are following the Intent of your body.
No direction> the Masses will just follow, don't you get it Yet?
Sheep led to the nuclear radiation chamber? Gluttons fed lies!
Halal Apocalypse, Kosher Armageddon, 'Holy' rivers of blood.
When is it your turn to jump out of Towers, resist these horrors?
Imprints of Information >:< affecting our children on Planet Earth

'Love is in the air'
Why give yourself a Hard time?
Polka dot mushrooms hard wired in the brain.
Impregnated in your caress; Let it grow & grow
Simple Minded dreamer by a river ~
Psychaos * Psychedelic * Psyche*delicious Psy * chics ~
Irritation, healing Sensations of your sensuous Awareness.
To make 'Surreality' not fruit salads of ananas, banality.
They're my teeth, why do you have to make a comment?
Living on the edge of a padi with roses & bougainvillea.
"I'm here to Please, I'm your man" Enjoying everything ~
Inquisition impulse, bring in the Converter; No Thank You!
Loving yourself, the images of that love being reflected ~
Staying in the wave because it's raining, a constant flow
You know how to die, Kundalini arising in a crystal Mirror.
I need a new thing, can you let the snake dance in trance?
I have to look through your eyes
Making love on Tibetan rooftops forgetting who you are.
*

In It to Win It
So many damaged people ~ trying to put on a happy face.
It's flowing through me & you, like a deranged Amazonian.
I'm not too much at home, you can make your own Choices.
A great time was had by all free, fornicating, passionate spirits
I'm walking my Enfield, through an Indivisible rainbow ~
Shit you're going to die, trepidation but then you made it!
You got good duality programs going through your tunnel.
To Know the Oneness ~ what's the Solution to Relativity?
Debt free, transmitting, burning the grain Human Patent.
The Picture's interesting but live it in the here and now ~
They just want to pull your heart out and constrict you.
"He still has a wall in his head" ~ dispatched to Siberia.
Going into his brain * to see what they think they know.
Found them lying in a Toxic dump of visceral Pollution.

Tribal Gift

Building this Higher * energy body
Playing in the swaying fields ~
Reconnecting * with our tube
Allowance ~ it becomes
What you give it
Who you are ~
Tuning into Rainforests
Reinforcing Consciousness
What is ready is being here now
*

Objective watching 'Zeitgeist'
The frequency of time ~
Smell the Roses
Shifting heavens
Translucent Life Force
Subjective diamonds on fire.
*

This Matrix Shop

One long high wave crossing the Ocean ~
They fooled us from the beginning, always on the hop.
Unripe Banana bullshit, China bought up America's shop.
Calling in the Big Debt,
start to sweat.
Mind Matter
Not the Master in the home ~
Instant Karma * tools of Intention.
Already there just Connecting
Breaking through firewalls of the Stoned age.
Reinforcing us * It's happening
Breathe taking in the Prana
Transmuting the dimension
Sacred Marriage * Spirit * Mother together
All that Happy horseshit

Triratna * (3 Jewels)
Taken from the Ivory coloured breasts of an Indian Princess!
Mahavira carried out of town (by the Gods) on a Palanquin...
Intending to renounce the World ~ composed a Sanskrit haiku.
Be careful what you dream for, making a wish can come True.
Woke up next to fertility Goddesses enjoying holy cunnilingus ~
We carved our names with hearts into a Kailasa Rock Temple
*

Asura Architect Maya
"Gave their power to the arrow ->
which alone could overcome the demons"
She fucked me by the Great Sun Temple of Konarak, Orissa.
A Queen from Gotland I found her to be perfect & super sexy.
We laid together naked, atop the wheel of a great Sun chariot,
entwined in the frieze of erotic groups of rampant, fertility deities
*

Unicorn in heat
A Unique Person
The harmony is flowing
"I can feel ~
what she feels
She feels
what I feel"
*

Haiku Keys
Lots of knowledge in a few simple words
Hitting the Point ~ with surrealist allegory.
Everyone knows about Banana bullshit...
Makes no sense ~ making complete sense!
You're Living your dream * No Mind * In Mind.
Same Same, just games of emotional addiction,
evolution but different, is it implying detachment?
False illusions appear ~ Separating the Lie.
Fractal < All * One > Freedom

"Hey Fucker Sit Still!"
Hawaii, some ugly spirit of America is dominating her ~
Tata Metal Works bought it, just destroying the Earth!
These are the moments when you say nothing or not.
Enjoying it for what it is ~ villagers getting no peace
Stop thinking about it, who cares?
A Love going to sleep in that wave ~
From the Mind of a Polynesian Warrior
I Got my daughter!

*

A 10 Rupee Riot
Shows you how brainwashed I am & I'm not even drunk!
It wasn't actually what I read, it was the reading itself ~
Gripping a fag; holding onto the remote control, onto life!
The male ego flash; came on a falling star, trillions of digits.
Good to go crazy, hey man you lost it! "Peace is Important"
Going through the storm into your next bespoke Boxed-set!
A Mystical lingham, an experience you'll never ever forget,
don't be too fixed with Judgment, be flexible, adaptable.
Not addicted to dogma, principles, keepin' it flowing....
We don't want to go to Siberia, freezing in an Icy gulag!
No separation, All allowance, acceptance, fine tolerance.

*

Neo-Labour, fascism's 3000 new laws in their first ten years!
Mould, reshape, brainwash, socially engineering their society.
Their responsibility taking us into an imposed 'Paranoid reality'
"You're not allowed to do this or that without dire results ~ "
'Can't escape the Database' locked up dodging a TV. License!
A Criminal Offence, left your bin lid open 4 inches! Depression.
Yet they gave the greedy Banks £50 Billion in a credit crunch!
Officially calling the Dalai Lama a Separatist and a Terrorist!
Blink, realise this is Not a dream, you are being hypnotised.
Your Brain/Mind is being manipulated into a compliant state.
It's not a conspiracy theory, look at those living around you!

It's alive and flowing ~ cause and effect…
Fear not to have enough money, stuck in duality.
"You spent so much Energy" & Synchronicity?
"Liberation is not upset by Happiness or distress"
A Consciousness that can't remember ~ itself,
too frightened to open the curtains for a peak.
Everywhere is good if you have the choice.
Are we falling asleep while we're awake?
"I could Live here, a place called Paradise"

*

Catalyst On Your Wavelength
"You don't have to drink to Party"
Pranayam cappuccinos on Ayuhuasca Day.
An Original Life ~ No Clinging Please
"I need a Spaceship ready for the sky"
Truly ~ There are humble people here.
'You are the Star coming from the Stars'
Mental (full) double trouble bubble Baba.
"Everybody's gotta get paid even the extra aliens"
Jewelry of an Illusion, putting Shiva into practice.
LSD. the Master of illusion, seeing All delusions.

*

This is it
So you're in Love with an Automaton, Android!
They shoot deserters don't they at the crack of dawn?
'Our systems have detected unusual traffic from your network
we're checking if this is really you sending requests or a Robot'
Fail Safe, Defrag * Haywire * rewire
Scramble, Initiate the Kill switch
Strap her into Artificial Intel!
That's a Live weapon!
Who wants to Live?

Civil Courage

People have to have the Guts to be themselves
A misunderstanding but also a lesson.
Fell under the Spell
I don't want to come in with my Mind
'Realising it ~ Is getting it'
Never seeing her frequency before ~
Working from the other side Bringing it over ~
Leaving her body in a beautiful green summer dress
Recalling the smell of the Ocean

*

Switch * Pineal

She's there to put her in your Heart
Discernment & get It ~ in the Imprint
Transmuting in the Chakras ~
Allowing Yourself to see Your*Self.
Seeing from every position
Reference Point >My Self < Point of Discernment
+ - 0 ~ & All the Colours of the kaleidoscope.
Jumping to different positions in the matter.
Being in the Shoes of another for empathy.
Mingling with your frequency ~
No matter what the friction and game.
Step Higher

*

Such A Fool's Paradise

The Officer failed the security test! 423,000,000 miles to Land
on Mars or for them to have Landed at Atlantis one sunny day
"Winners make the Rules losers live by them"
"Israel has at least 150 Atomic weapons" says Jimmy Carter;
Palestine, "One of the greatest human rights crimes on Earth"
We know irrefutably humans still behave not as noble savages.
Yes! Need to face facts, reflections on the processing of death.
"Where Ignorance is bliss it is folly to be wise"

Delight It with natural Light
Partying Inspiration, philosophical*spiritual*no words, vortices.
Experiences * Health of a body, tuning into others' vibrations.
Relating ~ Potential for addiction * Obsession, compulsions.
Potential for everything to be good, bad, non linear, quantum.
Depends on the Illusions of the Illusion of your mind in Space.
2000 People off their heads at Hilltop enjoying, feeling energy.
Paranoiac or Shamanic ° Tantric mantra ° Zany through Zen ~
Context of Identifications, prejudices, fears, selfish desires etc.
Why make such a big deal of things? Aware of Your Sense self.

*

Flower Malas of Itinerant Bards
Expansion of Mind * Enhancing of feeling, rising of Passion.
Conspiracies - What is the Truth from your own Experience?
"You are a Chemical Reaction in my brain of an Illusion ~
I am a chemical reaction in your brain which is a process"
But we don't realise it but Identify with the creation of an ego.
"We don't play by the rules" keeping up hypnotic rhythms ~
A moment of Recognition

*

Stoned * A 200 Rupee fine story
Slows down time so you can see more ~
A Goddess riding a tiger having a sunset drink with me.
"They're mad, what do you do to get back into control?"
They love gadgets and waffle makers ~
She was privileged to meet a Caveman.
Full Baba ~ turning up at your Front door!

*

Feels
In Monsoon time
We're rather Serene.
I'd want to be Clear ~
took a Microdot and missed the lunar eclipse
I wanna fly!

A Hitler Lock
Smoke screen not coming up in the bright Sunshine.
Client of Weapons or expert to a Marijuana grower.
"I always like to meet Queens of the Aureole Islands"
Streamin' her delicious strawberry auroras & energies.
'Waiting on the girls from Bangaluru'
"I don't wanna say goodbye yet"
Shaking Jungle, entanglement.
What to do without the Mother?
Follower of light angels
Creation is already there ~
Organic Looking for Something
Looking for Something to Find.
Have to break ~ all the rules
The Process ~ being so Obvious
Unreal layers * living masks
Myths of Fabulous Creatures.
"What's It got to do ~ with You?"
"Goin' to go ~ flippo here.
Woke up in a very strange mood, did his Puja.
"You have to go ~ to the Source"
'What's it ~ all about?'
5* Asylums of Addictions
of the deep hooks
of the flipping Into ~
With the Acceptance
*

Up Another Yangtze with little Buddhas
'Over the wavy Ledge!' There is no edge ~
Purple haze, Strawberry fields, Blue Clear, Hofmanns, Shivas,
California liquid Sunshine, White Lightning, Black Microdot,
Superman, Ganesh, Hendrix, Marilyn Monroe, Dolphins.
'Niketeta' ~ Innocence, magnificence
Courage from the Heart

41

The Best Namaste
Perfect Place In a Storm ~
Hari Krishna, League of Devotees.
Some Gurus move in ~ Air Con. Mercs.
Came lookin' for Shiva found Govinda.
Leaving the dancer behind
Becoming one with the Divine
"You can't go into trance in a lick her bar"
Trance is mystical * no head banging!
Spiritual stuff ~ tuning into the whole.
*

Full Thor
The Moon in Venus.
Do Sadhus take Acid?
Nice & Spiritual
in the mountains, Parvati Valley.
Are you sure it wasn't all a dream?
Taking Samadhi in a white quartz cubist Sphere.
Angel on a motorbike
"And I saw her"
*

Slapstick
"Did me the World of Good,
made me chuckle"
Putting Love into the Soil, collective conscious
Causing no distress
That seems Spiritual for our age.
Captain. Methrie dancing away all our karmic pain.
Frustration, seeing it only as Cosmic sensation ~
Time for Men
to prostrate harmoniously
In front of Venus

Businessman's link to the Blossom!
Like a dog with a collar on a Big metal chain.
Focusing on the Spiritual in the moment ~
In a Boutique Whorehouse captivated by the moist Craic.
Satsang of non ~ existential Indian Science fiction writers.
White Tantra Magic running through this Cosmic cartoon
All a reflection of Yourself
Allowing it to happen
Outside reflects what the Inside needs
Transmutation as above so as below ~
The Mind's desire for what it already has.
We allow ourselves to appreciate this instant.
The Mind thinks ~ Given up with the question.
Floating to 1000 petalled flowering Lotuses
Whole state of Ego is a sinking ship
Get in the lifeboat!
All the good properties are being snatched up!
In the middle witnessing the present moment ~
Is only the gift out of yourself, you give yourself.

*

Love Palace
Reflection of what I can experience ~ If I want to…
The lighter it got the higher I got beyond the fluffy clouds;
super clarity, I could see beautiful, kaleidoscopic orbs!
We're already there, It's alright from wherever we come.
My feelings, being very emotional, It's all inside ourselves

*

Throbbing Nuclearist
SLAVE STROKING HER Engorged HOOD.
Lost all my money, absent Mind-memories!
"Power comes out the barrel of a gun!"
"I will not be owned by anyone"

Changing Nature
Meditating All Around the World ~
Governing ourselves over the Internet cloud
If it's Cosmic it's Multi-dimensionality in Space.
Finding what's real ~ Pink blowjob puffer fish.
*Let's get it on one day * it's here right now!*
Transcending one's own fiction in the head
of the separated, Oneself; me reacting, Aware of ~
Conditioning, don't know who I am; I'm already here.
Presence of Intrinsic Space ~ Allowing it all to happen
Moments of pure formless consciousness
Don't relate to any FORM, the duality.
Into True Source of Life ~ Singularity.
Infinite is no beginning no end
*

No Red Carpet Sponsor
'Not Demoncrazy just Bureaucrazy' (Ask any 'Government')
Voting having any Choices, Autocrazy A or Kleptocrazy B?
Met a Baba at Ramjulla, swallowed it Hook line & Sinker!
We can, we can't help it sinking to the bottom of the river.
"Put your Mind inside your heart ~ your Heart in your mind"
Any crumbs they'll come for; Voracious appetites, Exactly!
Couldn't remember 24hrs before ~ liquid koshing of Libidos.
Full burning pyres of crony capitalism's sacrificial fires!
*

Bum Bolenath
Closest to the Garden
of Eden
Natural Paradise
It's all there ~
Then you find a cave
Then a Romantic, full dreadlocks caveman or cavewoman.
Stoned age, poetical dreaming is still alive.
But it's not a dream it's Real, Beautiful

44

In between breaks
Don't have to look at the a la carte menu...
Stopping children from chewing exotic viruses
Limiting the growth of the brain to critically 'THINK'
2009 only right to vitamins from a 'Codex' Witch doctor.
You Can't sell herbs, can't give Arnica, not Allowed by law!
Love potions Minimalised, Criminalised, bio-deMagnetised.
Everything under the skin goes into the blood stream.
You go to the medicine man ~ he gives you a Tattoo
brings out your full Force (In the Marquesas Islands).
DMT. in the Root Cortex of a favorite girlfriend!
Dancing with a Pomegranate ~ 'The Apple of Paradise'
Get good balance ~ of Anti Oxidants, full enzyme content.
*Krishna's Pleasure, **Incarnation of Pure Love,** smiling kiss.*
Put your full heat lips over this ~
*

The Smacked Accountant
Kali puts her shaved head between her hands. Top Goddess if you can see.
A Senior Pentagon, War Criminal, well connected to masked dictators.
Screaming banshees in Bedlam, retired to Fort Lauderdale, Florida!
'Madness Incorporated' - Controlled by a Plastic Card. Otherwise,
"S\he doesn't Exist" because doesn't have a Bank Account!
"Do you think anybody would waste Rohypnol on her?"
Look at that beautiful, sultry girl eating our digestives.
An Eco-Activst with Raw chocolate vapours.
It made me high, really biting into the cake!
*

ESquire
Where's my corn? Living in the pig pen covered in shit!
Making money for the Lord of the manor, it was all Fake News.
Not giving a fuck about anyone! "It's their way forward mate."
Baffling the people forever

Cosmic Flowers Blossoming

Thank You ~ Gratitudegratitudegratitudegratitudegratitude.
A Guise, "Back to work - I think I'm good for another year!"
She's not subservient as an oven, she's a Full power juicer!
It's not a problem for a plant to die ~ beyond thinking mind.
And dreaming into the present evolution * Spangled, twated,
old Acid Head with a senile dimension, completely wasted!
"You don't know you're a victim" it's Just a negative label.
"Wouldn't come here if it wasn't Insane, want to fuck my brain!"
Ingrained, creating a new Genesis, new Era, dump your baggage.
Lose 20kg. become a thin insomniac, speed freak at the Ice hotel.
Down at the 'Bad boy Bad girl Bar'
"Musically, true democracy because every note is equal"
Dionysus on dialysis at the National health cottage hospital.

*

Kama Sutra Yoga

69 Asanas with an Indian goddess talkin' doll
Thirty fingered, six armed Shiva
Polishing his Lingham

*

'Cosmos' Gk.~ 'Spirit of the World'

Pan Hazard Job Centre, "I have to do nothing to express myself" ~
I don't make myself Co-dependent on anything or anyone anymore.
"Today it's very difficult to know who is Stalin in Russia" ask wikileaks!
Making black Kali Chillums for Parvati's friends in a valley of flowers.
Duped, hired accidentally; no Judgment, old Ministry programming.
Guarding my heart when Spirit goes on holiday. Free let's see…
'They're not his creations, they're my ego Self-creations'
"I DON'T MAKE THE DAY * THE DAY MAKES ME"
Feel it * Heal it; have the Experience right now.
Getting lighter & lighter, higher & higher ~
Here It's only YES & Thank You, grazie, merci.

46

Tuning Tool
'Ugly Americanism at its worst'
All off their materialist heads!
Astronomical Brain, deranged!
It can get you onto which Moon?
Stay around awhile ~ Maybe?
'She'll come dancing out for you
Like the stars at night'
When it comes you know it's there.
Blasting-off from pussy pink Auroras
*

Fluffy Hallucinations
"It's more to do with being in tune"
Crystal clear, not giving a fuck conscious.
Hyperchondriacs.com in the first place.
The thing is Not to get in the shit
*

Tao Mountain
"Everything will be good!"
"I was just Shining"
*

Frisky Glasnost
'Shut the Mind Off' "Get in Line -
Welcome to the Food Chain Bitch!"
Stepping up to Maintain a Kyrgyzstani Supermodel.
Taking her under my wing.
Remixing 'California Dreamin' at Sunset beach.
"Black dudes all have nice fingernails in LA."
Ecstasy on a hot Tuesday afternoon In June.
Full flagrante delicto at the Eros Garden Centre.
Unfolding acid trips on a Cosmic, Oceanic ship.
Sacrificing a lemon on her vertical rainbow ~
'Don't Look back ~ at Love'

Chimps' Memory Banana
We shouldn't have come down out of the canopy!
'Mind or No Mind' ~ Witnessing the trees and the forest.
Relativity, duality or unity that is the question? Just Space.
*No More Toxic * Its Cosmic!*

*

Smiling Mama
Tripping on the chai mat by the sea.
The Pleasures of Time ~ Space
Not having 1000's of things
In my head

*

They know what's truth & lies.
'Drugs that money can't buy!'
Everything comes at the right time ~
after the plague was flushed downstream,
wanders into a beautiful, quiet, bamboo grove.
All religions trying to hold us static, all thought -
Forms when everything is expanding & growing!
It's hard to give it up, devoted to all their attention
to materialism, not growing anywhere, no trees left!
The Vatican holding up the lies, Cardinals in self ~
Hypnosis, Jesuits believing Lucifer; the lie that God
Is outside not inside & that Your God doesn't exist!
The victor continues to write their version of history!
The enemies of Love and compassion are numerous.

*

Sub-Prime, Ninja Loans - No Income, No Job, No Assets.
'8 people have as much wealth as half our planet's population'
Are you also an Inhuman Unsympathetic, Insatiable Sociopath?
'Tata Works' > Caste system, chain-gang on the roads.
*'Cos*money' > Confidence in the Illusion ~ of Economy.*
JewUSalem's Baron Rothschild, Investors in Global debt!
I know where it is but I didn't know what it was until now!

Wobbly Bob
More Shanti ~
Primal survivor
Swimming in the sea
with a python of gravity
Living on the wavy ~ edge.
That's why they gave you a Disabled badge.
"Go and see daddy"
"Don't make me a slave" ~ Beam me up!

*

Ayuhuasca ~ On the Rainbow diet
'Loanwalla' - getting loans made easy & sexy!
Poverty wipes out your morals real quick.
Sitting on the street drinking a Mai Tai,
watching people being mugged by the Police!
The Economy is collapsing, water wars, freaky patterns ~
Living in a cardboard box, lucky, too many people homeless!
Where is the balance, is there a balance for Mother Earth?
Choice; cheap ethanol for your car or feeding starving Darfur.
People drinking Biofuels, without Ice. What are we doing?
Everything goes up with the price of bread! Consequences.
The Rivers will dry up! Where is the realisation?
I wouldn't hold your breath ~
"The Sun is getting hotter darling"
Is this all bullshit just to get new higher Carbon Taxes?
Psychological Warfare! "We know the sea is coming"

*

Big surprise overtaking a holistic cow, from behind, thought
it was an Elephant on the road at night! And all these people
walking in unlit streets, dressed in black. Full beam headlights
glaring straight at you, running you off the road into a ditch!
Impossible trying to figure out that 'logic' as a Prime Target!
Integrated, Non-defensive ~ If only I could see into your Mind!

Quotes of Sri Nisargadatta

"We are the creators and creatures of each other, causing and bearing each other's burden." I find that somehow, by shifting the focus of attention, I become the very thing I look at, and experience the kind of consciousness it has; I become the inner witness of the thing. I call this capacity of entering other focal points of consciousness, love; You may give it any name you like.
Love says, "I am everything" ~ Wisdom says, "I am nothing"
Between the two, my life flows. Since at any point of time & space I can be both the subject and the object of experience, I express it by saying that I am both and neither and beyond both   (269)

*

Unless you make tremendous efforts, you will not be convinced that effort will take you nowhere. The self is so self-confident that unless it is totally discouraged it will not give up. Mere verbal conviction is not enough. Hard facts alone can show the absolute nothingness of the self-image.   (523)

*

A quiet mind is all you need. All else will happen rightly, once your mind is quiet. As the sun on rising makes the world active so does self-awareness affect changes in the mind. In the light of calm and steady self-awareness, inner energies wake up and work miracles without any effort on your part.   (311)

*

The world is like a sheet of paper on which something is typed. The reading and the meaning will vary with the reader, but the Paper Is the common factor, always present, rarely perceived. When the ribbon is removed, typing leaves no trace on the paper. So is my mind, the impressions keep on coming but no trace is left   (225)

*

When you demand nothing of the world nor of God, when you want nothing, seek nothing, expect nothing then the supreme state will come to you uninvited and unexpected   (195)

"There is no such thing as a person. There are only restrictions and limitations. The sum total of these defines the person. The person merely appears to be, like the space within the pot appears to have the shape and volume and smell of the pot. By all means attend to your duties. Action, in which you are not emotionally involved and which is beneficial and does not cause suffering will not bind you. You may be engaged in several directions and work with enormous zest, yet remain inwardly free and quiet, with a mirror like mind, which reflects all, without being affected." (50)

*

"To expound and propagate concepts is simple, to drop all concepts is difficult and rare" "There is nothing to practice ~ To know yourself, be yourself. To be yourself, stop imagining yourself to be this or that. Just be. Let your true nature emerge. Don't disturb your mind with seeking" ~ I am that

*

In people with devotion, even with limited intellect the intellect is not making mischief, as it is here. This is the place where the intellect gets annihilated. Consciousness and the Absolute.

*

There was a house, and in the house there was a person; now the person is gone and the house is demolished. The sum total is whatever experiences you have, whether for a day or for years it's all illusion. The experiences begin with knowingness. What is the most ingrained habit you have? It is to say 'I Am' This is the root habit. Words and experiences are unworthy of you. This habit of experiencing will not go until you realize that all this domain of the five elements, are unreal. This 'I Amness' is itself unreal. The un-manifest manifested itself, that manifest state is Guru and it is universal. Who is the one who recognizes this body-mind? This 'I Am-ness' which recognizes the body ~ mind
**is without name & form ~
it is already there**

<u>Hindu Glossary Arranged from Sri Nisargadatta Maharaj</u>

Advaita: *Non-duality,* **Adya:** *Primordial, original.* **Agni:** *Fire.*
Aham: *I, the ego.* **Ajnana:** *Ignorance.* **Akashaa:** *Ether.*
Ananda: *Bliss, happiness, joy.* **Asana:** *Posture, seat.*
Ashram *Hermitage.* **Atma:** *The Self.* **Avatar:** *Divine incarnation.*
Bhagavan: *The Lord.* **Bhajan:** *Worship (of the Lord).*
Bhakti: *Devotion, love (of God).* **Bija:** *Seed, source.*
Brahman: *God as creator.* **Brahma-randhra:** *Opening in the*
crown of the head. **Buddhi:** *Intellect.* **Chaitanya:** *Consciousness.*
Chakra: *Plexus.* **Chit:** *Universal Consciousness.*
Chitakasa: *Mental ether (all pervading).* **Chitta:** *Mind stuff.*
Deva: *Divine being.* **Dhyana:** *Meditation, contemplation.*
Ganapati: *A Hindu deity, success-bestowing aspect of God.*
Gayatri: *Sacred Vedic mantra.* **Gita:** *Song.* **Guna:** *Quality born*
of nature. **Guru:** *Teacher, preceptor.* **Hanuman:** *A powerful deity.*
Hatha Yoga: *A system of Yoga for gaining control over the*
physical body and Prana. **Hetu:** *Cause, reason.* **Hiranyagarbha:**
Cosmic intelligence, Cosmic mind. **Iswara:** *God.* **Jagat:** *World*
changing. **Jagrat:** *Waking condition.* **Jiva:** *Individual soul.*
Jnana: *Knowledge.* **Kalpana:** *Imagination of the mind, creation.*
Kama: *Desire, lust.* **Karma:** *Action.* **Karta:** *Doer.* **Kendra:** *Centre,*
heart. **Kriya:** *Physical action.* **Kumbhaka:** *Retention of breath.*
Kundalini: *The primordial cosmic energy located in the individual.*
Laya: *Dissolution, merging.* **Lila:** *Play.* **Linga:** *Symbol.*
Maha: *Great.* **Mahattava:** *The great principle.* **Manana:** *Constant*
thinking, reflection, meditation. **Manas:** *Mind, the thinking faculty.*
Manolaya: *Involution and dissolution of the mind into its cause.*
Mantra: *Sacred syllable or word or set of words.* **Marga:** *Path or*
road. **Mauuna** *or* **Mouna:** *Silence.* **Maya:** *The illusive power of*
Brahman, the veiling and projecting power of the Universe.
Moksha *or* **Mukti:** *Release, liberation.* **Mula:** *Origin, root, base.*
Mumukshu: *Seeker after liberation.* **Murti:** *Idol.*
Nada: *Mystic sound.* **Nadi:** *Nerve, psychic current ~*

Namarupa: Name and form, the nature of the world. **Neti-neti:** "Not this, not this" negating all names and forms in order to arrive at the eternal underlying truth. **Nirguna:** Without attributes. **Nirgunabrahman:** The impersonal, attributeless, Absolute. **Nirvana:** Liberation, final emancipation. **Nirvikappa:** Without the modifications of the mind. **Niskama:** Without desire. **Para:** Supreme, other. **Parabrahman:** The Supreme, Absolute. **Prajna:** Consciousness, awareness. **Prakriti:** Causal matter, also called Shakti. **Pralaya:** Complete merging, dissolution. **Prana:** Vital energy, life breath. **Prema:** Divine love (for God). **Puja:** Worship. **Purna:** Full, complete, infinite. **Purusa:** The Self which abides in the heart of all things. **Rajas:** One of the three aspects of cosmic energy, passion, restlessness. **Sadhana:** Spiritual practice. **Saguna - brahman:** The Absolute conceived of as endowed with qualities. **Sakti** or **Shakti:** Power, energy, force. **Samadhi:** Oneness; here the mind becomes identified with the object of meditation. **Samsara:** The process of worldly life. **Samskara:** Impression. **Sankalpa:** Thought, desire imagination. **Sat:** Existence; being; reality. **Sat chit ananda:** Existence - Knowledge - bliss. **Satsang:** Association with the wise. **Satva** or **Sattwa:** Light; purity. **Siddha:** A perfected Yogi. **Siddhi:** Psychic power. **Sphurna:** Throbbing or breaking forth; vibration. **Sunya:** Void. **Susumna:** The important nerve current that passes through the spinal column through which the kundalini rises. **Susupti:** Deep sleep. **Swarupa:** Essence; essential true nature of Being. **Tattva:** Element; essence; principle. **Turiya:** Superconscious state. **Vairagya:** Indifference toward all worldly things. **Vasana:** Subtle desire. **Vichara:** Inquiry into the nature of the Self. **Vijnana:** Principle of Pure intelligence. **Virat:** Macrocosm, the physical world. **Viveka:** Discrimination between the Real & the unreal. **Vritti:** Thought-wave; mental modification. **Yoga:** Union; Patanjali's philosophy of the union of the individual with 'God'. (Cosmic ~

Jade a Green Jewel
Out of body ~ out of Mind.
Forever Strawberry fields,
Blue Cheer * Purple haze.
Then I hit the liquid
Blew my brains
Not Thinking ~
Just doing it, being it
A good night that!

*

Still Legal Spiral
A Seed is a Seed, no THC. CBD. STP.
You can't hide behind a DMT. fiery bush.
Catalyst ~ Clashing with a Visionary Egg
To make a Life
"We're all spiritual ~ But divided by Religions"
Dead on the burnt out Sun bed ~
Monsoon, fishing for lush resonance
Less distractions * Cosmic Romance

*

Trance
No Words ~ realm of silence
You're with your own sounds
Samadhi music allows you to ~
Transcendence of the Release; bullshit.
Putting the paradigm ~ into magic spells.
'Knowing the Unknowable again'
You have to get out of the 'Rules' dimension.
A dusty crystal freaking out! 'I am Nothing ~
Same Same Same Same ~ nobody can hide.
Gathering by the Spirits, seeing more light
Suddenly a door ~ will Open for You
going to run ~ right in

Sod's law please

"He was still rogering her when the airport taxi turned up!"
Fun Time - Who's going to the Dubai Shopping Festival?
None of the 3 billion+ people living on less than $2 a day!
'St Anthony's Fire' - Pull 'em off the pyre, they're involuntarily
tripping through hallucinatory scenes à la Hieronymus Bosch!
Got some natural Ergot, ingredient in LSD * psychedelic bread.
"You are a little Planet in Space"

*

A Sacred Pyramid

Billy Graham; Where's the Spirit ~
Exploding into another dimension!
Showed me a book 'Practical Demon Keeping'
Are they on the New vine?
Mystical foundation can't put it into words.
"I went AWOL; took me off my ship ~
sent me to Live on a submarine in Hawaii!"
Who would really want to hurt anyone?
A common slave, give me 1.5 lakh
and I'll put him on the Police Force!
Release it, Stop the Mind's # Unconscious movements.
You have to tell > the Mind to 'Shut the fuck Up'
Expand your Pure consciousness ~ listening to Music.
Observing as the Experiencer <:> being the Allowance.
Knowing the 'Tree of Knowledge'
Judgmental, which is death; good or evil?
Witnessing, living integrated as the 'Tree of Life'
Not in parameters but freestyle, no separation.
"Yoga is discipline * Tantra is Integration"
Everywhere in the presence of the present

*

Magic
With Children ~ Enormous Fun

55

'Drinking Whiskey Driving Risky'
He ordered Chocolate Mousse, she brought Apple Crumble.
"I ordered chocolate mousse" "I know"
"We don't have any"

*

The Enfields just started turning up
The Light streaming through your eyes darling ~
Timeshare, "You've won a Ukrainian dream bride"
Believing in the Temptation and the Winning...
A corrupt Casting Agent; what did you expect?
And they say, Krishna said it was inclusive, True.
Channeling beyond the money, material energy...
There's not the answer, looking in the wrong place.
You've won the lottery in India, "It was Me, me, me!"
Your number's come up, giving thanks to Lakshmi!

*

Feeling It works ~ It is working
Killing & Killed for your Pre-Conditioned Mind-set.
Medieval system of Control, Machiavellian Role!
Playing with a goal in view, out of step with now.
No future no past ~ Unfolding, Instantaneously.
We are the Infinite Source
There is No separation
'Everything is part of 'you'
You are part of Everything'
Perfect game over, nothing left to aim for.
On a level above the thinking level ~
'Authorities' not allowing you to glide over Mount Kailash.
Nomads wind surfing in the Sahara with African telepathy.
Realisation can come from full loss ~Totally, Exactly!
You can see it's all bollocks sitting around a campfire.
Close as he could get to divine, crystal children.
What are you waiting for? Channeling Paradise

<u>Sweet lassies & Greek Japes</u>
"Rattled her on the beach, went out on the lash.
She did the washing up, the pots and ironed my clothes!"
Kama Sutra Yoga; "Somebody's in for a treat!"
Kiss of a Snake ~ 'Just at one with them all'
"I don't know what it is ~ but I got It"

*

<u>Frequencies of the Sun</u>
*The Living Proof * A Living Legend, Iconic.*
We're all Babes in the eyes of the Universe
Partying since the Stone age. The Bad old days, burning
Eve at the Stake; chopped off another Consort's noggin!
No goin' back, it's all within.
'Noblesse Oblige' ~ 'Privilege entails Responsibility' oh yeah!
Ethiopians on the dark Ether-Net setting up deals for a 'Coffle'
Train of beasts ~ slaves fastened together. Unbelievably true!
Everyone can be who s/he wants to be ~ Accepting Happiness.
Not Guilty for feelings of having Fun, fancy free.
Detached self, so no problem, no victim, easy.
Lights up like a big glowworm in heat ~
Losing your rights, what do you know?
Leave it to the Universe ~
Chimps in trees with tomahawks; now I know the ropes!
*How to see with your Heart * more & more feeling*
*Open * Portal for the docking Soul.*
Receiving ~ Akashic Information

*

<u>You're a FREE WO*MAN</u>
You're not legally Obliged to do anything, Know Your Rights!
When they put on that uniform they have duties & responsibilities.
*Your Birth Certificate incorporated you ~ "I'm a Living Wo*man."*
You are a Live birth going into the 'Illegal system'; it's by Consent!
You are the Executor means you are the Beneficiary not a Trustee.
The Queen is my Trustee, she's there to protect my rights me Lud!

Rainbow Fractals
You allow the Space for a Crystal Temple ~
The Programmer's picture of a Merkaba in flight.
I know in my heart, Invocation of the five Dakinis.
Taliban using Heroin for Jihad, have to shoot it up!
Can't see what good it did for them, intent on suicide.
A real weapon of Mass Destruction; Fuck off, fuckwits!
Shouldn't be stoning people; buying a slave in the market.
*

Focusing their energies, drugs, the liquid Kosh.
'If only people could Live in the Heart'
Global ecosystem, no borders, no limits ~
Goddesses around you, more the merrier.
'No Money, No Honey darling'
Life Sharpens the Razor's edge.
Fuelling the War on drugs, protesters taking LSD.
Authority Outlawing them, Chaos in the Mandala
*

Perfect Finish
We don't have to sell ~ ourselves any more.
You Are the Gift
Already
*

"Pressure is there!"
'The latest Invaders of India'
"Less speed, less tension, more speed more tension."
'The Super dense Crush Load' - Over packed & over here!
"I grew up homeless in Howrah" ~ "not a care in the World"
A favourite destination for runaway kids for decades!
Free to be Your Self, praying to Shiva every moment.
"Get hit by a train and go straight to the End"
Durga our Patron Saint riding on a Super Loco.
Removing the Obstacles on the line!

Drunken Skinheads
Those Indians! Offensive, rude; wants to make them Insane.
Greedy ego bringing them Hip Hop with Alcohol & Cocaine!
Psy*trance with the Acid in more intelligent musical spheres.
"They'll eye you more, they'll try you more"
Guaranteed to all kick off!
*

Lethal Stela
They call it ~ 'Wife beater'
"What are you doing?" "Gotta pick up stuff!"
Give it from the heart not tempted by the bubblegum.
Picking up one Paranoid blink, got no chance!
"Giving them what they want to see"
*

Fields of Peaceful Protons
The Love that fills you up * the 'Real You'
Recognising Yourself in everything else
In the Vibrating Temple of your heart.
Looks like everywhere else but here!
The future coming as the Present flow ~
Tactics of the Mind to escape the beingness ~
Needs a Sense of Time to manifest in the Space.
You can truly only 'make a Plan' ~ for right Now.
Enjoy this Moment ~ It Never Stops changing
*

All in the Cerebellum
Mantras from your Mind ~ "In Spirit there is No caste"
Free from Mind-body-heart-sense paradigms
What's left? Just You infinitely whole....
*

Get a Grip!
"Ain't no Love like your Love"
Throbbing lingam on her hip, cheeks, lip to lip.
Person to Person ~ Face to Face

<u>For the Best of Hari Krishna</u>
Sinking, No Thinking ~ Trained like dogs.
Reward or Punishment * The Mind State!
Unconscious Moments ~
Bird flying to a branch
You Are This Space
Ego exists from a Point of Separation
If you pull it into the light
It doesn't exist
Blocked by rushing to get to the future!
The Mind is part of the Consciousness
Thinks I've got it Now…
Being here ~ experiencing what Is existence
If there was no Space there'd be no 'Mental-Form'.
Are you a Fractal, is she in love with a hologram?
Listening to the silence
You know you're doing what you wanna do
*

Driving yourself Mad!
Mind Your-self in eternal Space.
Ego demon of darkness ~
Sita with a heart of devotion
Ram * Ram
*

DMT; PMT. give them the extra bottle!
There's a bag of coke under that Robe.
Earth Sky Pixie ~
"Absolutely Goa"
Fall into Creation
Creativity flowing through You & me.
Revelation is all ready ~
to tune in and to give.

Adopting Ganesha
1kg. of Passion fruit; building frames of reference.
"We've lost completely the feeling of our animals."
Cosmic Bob with Pop Up Bill
Big hookahs in there, daft as a brush.
Laughing too much to Myself ~
broke a rib, couldn't stop,
Is there anything better?
I lost the Plot, "Shalom, Chillum Central"
I like Radha, Laxmi, Parvati, Rukmini, Priti, especially Rati,
& Saraswati playing music nicely, sitting on her white swan.
What to say Capt. Beefheart? "It makes sense in the moment"
What to say Joe Strummer, about this Clash ~
How long in the Wilderness?
*

Reality Relationship
If You Allow for Observing Multi-dimensionality ~
No Identity, No defining, No Judgments, No Matrix, No Ego.
See it's always changing ~ Free flow ~ you have to let her go!
Of course no remorse and leave it consciously to the Universe
*

Yes Yes Yes
Automatic GPS * It's Great, You can turn Off Your willed Brain.
Take the Wrong Turn ~ It Recalculates exactly where you are!
Subjective Identity ~ Ignorance of Separation, duality.
Pure Consciousness ~ Trust, Trust, Trust grooving.
Let the Spirit flow through you & listen to what you say.
Bring it out ~ over your boundless beingness
Only how you perceive it ~ courage of heart.
Directly go in the feeling
of being connected, carried in the light net.
How you want to be in it ~ 'You are it'
'You Are You'

Serving a Blood Stream
Particles * dancin' ~
with light, noting else there.
You have to make a move
Have to have the Intention
for the Universe ~
to Open its doors.
'It is What it is'
It's not 'Going' ~ anywhere!
Flowing with the flow ~
_*_

Addictive Venom
Getting into the habit...
watching HD. Plasma TV.
Virtually Living Like This ~
Before I had to think about it!
'Ignorance' ~ Streams of nonsensical unconsciousness.
Mind's Projections got us into Moon orbit, on our Screen?
Brains like to go on holiday somewhere Sunny ~
On a hilltop with Psychedelic coloured Palm trees.
_*_

Vicious Circles
Out of The 'System'
floating above
the dancers
Creating your own
'Reality' ~
Gazing at Audio Hallucinations
_*_

Tarzan's Honour
They haven't got over the shock of what came after the hippies.
Offering flowers instead of Secret Society's satanic rites and rituals.
'The hammock generation' ~ Super Ego is more than Life to some!
I'm not in charge, Life's in charge

Talking to
Your * Self
In a field of energy
In a field of light
in an orange orchard ~ Lovely Portal
Only being here now is fulfilling
*
Bella-figura

Fractals * My eyes are open on the way home!
Royally f.....d 'Keeping them more than happy!
You've said it Yourself.... Everything is a lie!
Your whole life is a Massive PSYOPeration.
Super party everyone was off their heads!
It won't happen to me again because I know.
It's just a thought ~ How easy is it to change!
Reclaim your mind, redacted, unravelling its matrix.
Having another, new, different thought & sensation.
Is there any logical interpretation for your depression?
Having a thought that makes you smile ~ switches it Off!
We have a right to be here * millions of years of evolution,
before we knew how to make fire and we forget all of this.
The plants told me where to find the Birds of Paradise ~
*

Doesn't Gloria have a brain?

Mimicry and mockery; torture how much can you tolerate?
He's spreading the seedless from a loveless marriage.
You get married because you wanted to get married ~
When you separate that must be right too; be the witness.
You didn't give her what she wanted so she fucked off!
"You have a God given right to enjoy your life." she said,
then dumped me in the street with a mean look in her eye.
"Judge us not for our weakness but for our Love"

New Global Co-habitation Allegations

Found them battered in the Madhethe 'Interrogation Centre'.
Name of your House of Swords, the shaking bullies of Riyadh.
Dysfunctional Insanity! Hung him upside down, beaten with an
axe handle for weeks, friend being gang raped in the next room.
(State security detention)! Monsters driven in Golden carriages.
Their ancestors pitched their tents on an oil well, then sold it all
to Shell becoming super wealthy and giving them rights to hold
Mother Earth to ransom! USA on the moon, Soviets stuck a flag
in the Arctic ocean floor. Does it mean they own Our global ~
natural resources? Ask the gang-raped Qataf girl about justice!
Years worth of blood on floors of Swordid abattoirs, Undetected.
Holds a Koran in hand; whose survived these torture chambers?
Females can't leave the house without male guardian control.
No passport, not even allowed to drive a Mini Moke, not a joke,
even in a Medical emergency ~ but Praises our foreign Queen!
Doing business with your enemy. What's True, Real? Ask Miss
Badri al-Bishar. Sharia Judge asked if she was wearing her veil
(whilst being violated), then he acquitted her rapists! It's a Posse
of uniformed thugs ~ A Dictatorship of Absolutely no Democracy!
'The Commission for The Promotion of Virtue and Prevention of Vice.'
Gigantesque Hypocrisy giving £billions to Islamic Wahabbi extremists.
Corruption, hush money, signing cheques for misogynists and terrorists!
Yet these bankers ride in armored Limousines, keeping it sweet for him
and her in a depraved relationship with a tribe of Tyrants. Diverting the
attention of Muslims from all these activities of Swordid's Royal Dynasty,
with lots of skeletons in their oily desert. Fanatic visions eradicating all
their mystics. No one says Boo! Need to get a grip of your Criminalised
Addictions. Sycophantic - Arms deals for crude oil spilling blood on toxic,
gold banquet plates. Licked up by unscrupulous Government leaders, big
Arms dealers. BAE. paying $billions over 20 years to bribe Shaking snakes.
Who tells UK's Prime Sinister to stop its Serious Fraud Office's investigations
or Moslem terrorism will soon be arriving at a station near you?
Obviously Political Hypocrisy, lies, coercion, greed and Power!

<u>Soul brother to a King</u>
Everyone is allowed ~
As long as you don't hurt anyone.
Many people behind bars in America
You have to go out of the Emotions.
"I had great times in Prison"
Standing with People who are not broken

*

<u>A Rationalisation</u>
Doing it for Realisation not for Ego-Centrism.
You want to see what you want to see.
You can say anything if it's True.
Life Lived not just Information ~
If you see that you get the Reflection
In the other one
You can still smile ~ that's good
Learning, about to Trust
Then suddenly we came into another time ~
Wanting to feel something that was Real
Completely here & now

*

"I see an Indigo Rocket and I'm in it"
A thread with all the jewels of Life
Giving it to all the Divine ~
Going to Heaven
The Meditation that makes you Meditative.
Got the connection to her light work
Embodying a High Potential
Spreading energy ~ fast flowing Stream of Love.
Face to face with Fear, it falls of its own accord.
Radiating Love
Just you reflecting Your Innocence
Projecting fear in your Makeup mirror.
"The more you fear me the more terrible I become"

Chatting to the birds in India

Living totally Non Conventionally, Non Formatted ~
"Is there anybody out there?" We're all being Channelled.
Filters tuning it out, receiving all of it ~ to tuning it in now.
Are people feeling empowered? Don't need Masters on Top
Telling You When and how to live, what to do, what Not to do.
It's Your Responsibility, herding those bleating as sheep.
Tapping into the sub-conscious ~ 'I don't know', 'I believe'…
but I liked to hear it all until transcending this illusory bullshit.
Cryogenically sent to Mars preserved on a red hot Atoll.
Evolving through the Flood, no food, no water just Acid reign.
20 years standing on his head, visiting him in his dreamtime.
Ripped his Mind apart, opened up 1000 yellow Lotus petals.
"Shiva shit on you!" Corrupt Authorities' corrupting the life!
Building up your own Awareness of total Truth, of Dhamma.
You are even more Sensitive than a pill; Open your 3rd eye ~
This is Shiva * this is Shakti, sitting in the middle of a Torrent
Chanting mantras, watching the Devas waking up to rhythm.
Taking a leap of faith ~ have to climb our own mountains
*

In the Sun

Mind Playing Tricks * Special crystal spinning tetrahedrons.
Directly flowing, Allowing Yourself to be Yourself.
No more Judging ~ Inner Knowledge
Tuning Psychics, enjoyment, Celebrate. Hanuman said ~
"It fell down, it fell apart; You make your own experience…
Every moment you Create, this feeling, the Guru, the Spirit is
always with you; Going Somewhere, Can't Go back." I expected
people to be Conscious; why did you do that? I never Promised
anything. Fool's Gold, Full Speculation. Ego Attack, Ego divorce,
Ego frenzy, Ego Reaction, No Ego! Just step outside, flow inside,
surrendering right to be ~ 'Unconscious', give it up! Staying with
you, be Yourself. You are your Lover, first to Love ~ the other.
Energy rising through the Antioxidant Golden gates.

Barefoot in the Moonlight
Relativity of the chakras' vibrations ~
Did it work for you? Keys to enter this Universe
Visualising Geometric Form-patterns of humans on Earth.
Electrons spinning at the speed of light around a neutron ~
Darling your body's energetic field * sequencing you in tune.
A Mathematical code of Realisation in our multi*orgasms.
Program yourself; Activate your good Intention that counts.
Effective Micro-Organisms
*

Psyche*Sickness
Not in Synchronicity ~ balance
with vibrations of Mother Earth!
In * out of a time frame
Fully with you my 3D Star.
Fucking at the same speed ~
Recreating the Cosmic frequency
*

Getting in its place
Limited by the linear Gregorian calendar
While the Mayans are spiraling ~
Coming in time to the Galaxies'
Axis of the Pranic tube ~ in you darling!
Sitting with a poet in a Kashmiri flower garden
during an early, soft summer night.
Shiva's cosmic dancing ~ Tandava.
On the head of demons in a circle of fire
*

Discovered Compassion in my explorations not exploitations!
Bodhisattva left his sleeping, loving wife to renounce the World.
Yakshis riding on a griffin emerging from a dragon's mouth.
Came to a climax within a cloud maiden ~
Watching the wheel of law go up in flames
entwined in Loving embrace on a Lotus flower

Sonic Squat

You've no idea you're about to get killed!
Do you know Kung fu? Is it dangerous?
Paint your Oneness, people will recognise it.
When you compose the Truth, people will Listen.
Musing is suffusing ~ 'No Problems Only Solutions'
'Born crying, laugh dying'
Telepathic in tune with the Universe.
Dolphins and Whales singing
Shifting through dimensions
Crossing Oceans
*

Frequency 7

Plugging into light rays of Golden Topaz
Downloading * inconceivable Universes ~
Channeling ~ Reflecting all in the mirror.
Fully cleansing the Mind
through the aura fields.
Connected to the whole
In it all ready ~
Can't fall out of it
*

Sacred Geometry Exaltation

Flat on your back in Front of me ~ Points to her magic triangle.
Frees desire, "Please Fuck me on a Higher, Vibrational Level!"
Exhalation in our Pranic tubes, orgasms of exstatic Merkabas.
Energetic connection in our Inhalation * Qualities of Intention.
Solar Plexus penetration, females nourishing sweet temptation
Creates a blue Imprint in your Spiraling, golden heart of light ~
Feeling the Love of Father Sky ~ deep into your Mother Earth.
You're already an Angel of devotion; refreshing, nothing left to do

Agent Orange (Shiv Sadhu) Matrix!
Music taking my emotional body for an astral ride ~
Living in a circle of beauty together. In the moment,
not much to do. "Praise the Lord" fed by the Temple.
Switch into the 4th dimension, give it up to the others.
Sheltering in your Merkaba, spinning light in the Kasbah.
"I don't look back" for any explanation in the Mind's frames.
Higher guide for new world service. Tomorrow's not Important.
*Everyone is different, we are the metaphysical Christ * Crystal.*
Quality is fulfilling in the 3rd dimension ~ making spiral vortices.
Hooked up to Dualities, like & annoy, Adam & Eve, Roy & Joy.
Plugged in the sockets; Your kisses broke me ~ free

*

Orgasmic Coffee Offered to You
Who do we want to be? FULL ON ACID DROPS!
We make Programs, being in a Processing of duality.
*Key to discernment of the Mind * Inside the Polarities.*
Depending on how you swing it; Blonde Bombshells,
Baby is no business, throw it all in the seminal Ocean ~
Make a Fibonacci gem in the middle, walk away & have a joint!
Connection ~ Eyes opening up; it's not a forest but a tree farm.
Cut enough board length from Earth to Mars!
A dagger shoved into the heart of an angel.
All the Richness in Myself transmutating

*

Devotee's now
Celebrating the jewel of timelessness in Planets
Imprinting Implants, pregnant with consequences.
A volcano, hot under her shimmering magma bed.
*Twirling Lake Titicaca's quantum * biomagnets.*
When the Earth unfolds its Inside ~ Outside
*San Pedros * growing all over the Island.*
Going through the living on a beach trip.
Splitting up ~ time finding her own way

Acrobatic Yoga > Into thin air
Shovel it down your pants (got enough fossil fuel) at her coal face;
Why are they so shy? I felt the energy fields of open, Russian yoginis
(not Oligarchs). "You are already the gift" One thing is for everything.
Now ~ Living through humanitarian nightmares, do you Understand?
Another one on the burning horizon with innocent humans screaming!
No way of being ~ wrong or right, moving within limitless frequency.
Don't have to follow up the duality it's a spiraling 'Magic Roundabout'
Give yourself the Allowance, Space to accept yourself as you are.
Filled with all the Love of a purring Cosmos

*

Anticipation's Interpretation
Better Perception the better Reception > or hot Expectation!
Consumerism can it be real? Coke Zone, Who is Hypnotised?
'Share your things with everyone because you are everyone'
"Was Banned for 3 years for killing a pedestrian at 140 mph!"
Jumping out of it, see what you definitely don't want anymore.
Falling asleep but won't let go of the sole Remote Controller!
Waking up, keep on clicking the channels, to 'Lost in our Mind'
Unconscious dictator controlling the Social space, sitting there
watching any rubbish rather than go to bed; Light another fag!

*

A Nightmare down your street!
Decadence ~ L.A. women boxing in the nude; Slam wham bam!
You have the freedom to beat the shit out of your brains. Damn!
Not only that, they have a dwarf as the referee for equal rights!
Where's a point of Perversion? You're what you feed your Mind.
Who wants to go to an 'Altar Ego' Party at the Fetish Factory?
Entertaining the Crowd, breaking the Taboos at the Coliseum.
More Conditioning or De-conditioning ° finding the balances ~
Surviving Insane Caligula, not following the Queen, fuck it all!
Not invading or intruding into your place with my can of Mace.
Who wants to get battered? 'The knowing is already done!'
Now just presenting it, letting it be through you ~ creation

70

<u>No borders</u>
You could be the Poet Laureate from Norway.
"I'm from the FREE*World!"
Feeling light auras in Italian Love arias
Living like a Superstar ~ Laxmi Quality.
'Money with the Shanti'
Always look on it as your best friend ~
Not as hell; It can bring you great things.
A nice feeling ~ Right Peace of Mind.
Everything Perfectly * with that Angel!
Rich in Life ~ with everything you do
Contentment blessings
*

<u>Crystal Vibration</u>
They accused him of bad business practice
Giving everyone a PRISM Operating System.
'Light works on DNA, helixes creating your Hologram'
Of who we are ~ Shifting energy fields
"He's a 'Walk-in' from another Planet"
We are Cosmic
we are the other Planets!
We are Shiva
we are all the other Gods
*

<u>Then letting go</u>
Socrates lived by the beach & grew organic * il fungi magico *
Monkey with a number, they'll kill you with all their blessings!
'We have to make ourselves Conscious of this Consciousness'
She's from the Invisible Star of her seven sisters of Pleiades.
We're looking through a tiny, little window.
That's what we call, are told is our 'Reality'
Four years left to witness Goddess Venus.
Moving her body further away ~
Odysseys Into Deeper Space

<u>Cupid's * Vortex</u>
"What the fuck ~ are you doing?
Come to talk to my little polka dot blow fish.
They know each other ~ Alien the only friend
in town, exploded ~ was so smart and cute.
Lovers putting geometric codes into lights
The magic flute made up of triangles
Symbol of * a pure energetic marriage.
Colours on the streamers of Venus, her desirous heart.
Ravished by the fearful, dense consciousness of Mars!
The right use of Will ~ didn't listen to the power of 'No'
*

<u>Reading labias & sweating vulvas</u>
Ahead of their time * Evolution of a new race, non accountable.
A higher crime of conflict, Martian's logic had No Venus' feelings.
Activated right brain Lemurian ~ digital, violet grandchildren.
That energy Light knowledge, crystal pulsating communication.
The World is losing the Great Barrier Reef to resource exploitation!
I'M DOWNLOADING * UPLOADING NATURE.
This hanging on to Avarice gives us all Cancer!
Need to feel & heal our consciousness chakras.
Brought him to you to trigger the Transmission.
Affirmation, they want me on the free spirit road.
It's being here NOW ~ No other definitive code.
Otherwise too much Ego, too dense a load.
Got to keep the Meditation Space ~ No Mind.
Picking up the tools of the Cosmos
"That's how the Universe wants it"
If it's not mine ~ I don't covet other people's stuff.
She's got complete, immaculate Goddess energy
Seductive power; Not furniture to die for!
We shared the last rites, I was a gonna.
Resonating

'A penny for your thoughts'
Mind Does Not Exist, 'only In Reality'
That Magic touch ~ full Mental illusion!
Life is a body of sense consciousnesses.
Death is only a process of dying ~ change
Light left the body, *reflections of a galaxy.*
*Infinite Unity*Deepest Level of Co*existence.*

*

'Self-Appraisal'
Conversions, conventions of My fixed self, entity all delusions ~
Processing of God is a feeling in the heart, karma of Intentions.
He has no choice hanging on a Cross ~ look at your Motivations.
Throwing money changers out of the Temple à la Baron Rothschild!
How far can you run from the Imperial praetorian cohorts?

*

Live from the Heart
Cosmic cunnilingus in an angelic dimension ~
Anti-Gravity silver suits used for your Spaceship.
Preserving the live sperm bank in Om shanti hermitage.
Words have energy, synchronicity of clear windowpanes.
Embrace it, 'nothing's perfect' little green women synergy.
'The greatest deception is that closest to the Truth'
Wanting to be possessed by Spirit, looking in the wrong place.
*Step back from darkness, no to Absolute self be*Cosmic Space*
as creation goes back to natural functions of the Mind.
A programmed Mind, living next to a starving lioness!
'Nibbana's gates are open to everyone ~ '
Insightfulness into the nature of personality.
Lookin' free ~ More or less, just is, ever-changing nature.
Mother Earth's children, quest to Witness Mind's trappings.
You have to keep Giving, being, free of concepts, of dualities.
Where there's water ~ People have been going Out in boats.
Breast milk is a narcotic ~ fantastic for your baby.
Always wanting more & more!

Nothing to do with it
The Outside Group getting in touch ~ With the elemental
As soon as you go down you can go up too ~ being here now.
Trees show the electro*magnetic field; they want y/our energy.
Sugar the biggest drug, Underline <u>Drug</u>, Pharmaceutical CEO!
Without knowing it, trusting; you lobby, Doctor, Mr/s. Politician.
'A spoonful of Sugar Helps make the Medicine go down'.
He's enlightened now, since 2 days sees every rickshaw
differently, seen through the whole picture, on his knees.
Freedom of beingness, creating a home without even trying.
"I can let go ~ stretching out in the river of perfect allowance"
Looking him in the eye personally

*

Sweetness of Life
"A Gorgeous butterfly in a mini skirt with Big tits selling one cent
glasses of water on a busy, dusty corner, Bishkek, Kyrgyzstan"
Let's clean this energy, move on move on ~ into Paradise.
Letting go of what ^ they've been carrying for so long….
"I don't see the freedom in > Unjust Rules & Regulations!
Hitting a calf with a stick ~ that Time frequency.
How they Spin the whole Web ~ Worldwide!
All the Palaces, Castles will be destroyed.
The new Allowance is the next Golden Age.
Reflections of Unconditional Love Missions
The body is just a suit your Spirit will never die.
What frequencies are you holding In that body?
Holding it separately to Spirit ~
Clearing your own duality Perception, conception.
Logical Mind, mentally doesn't work in Zero Space ~
Effective Micro-Orgasms, did you get it or didn't get it?
They cut the DNA. System so we wouldn't understand anymore.
Celestial energy, diamonds evolving in crystals of pure Carbon.
Calculating it all by the Gregorian Calendar ~ Rivers of Grace
Rebuilding historical Time frames ~ that never ever existed!

Degaussing-Confusion-Infusion
Is a good state ~ they're going through
Relax with the lightning and thunder!
And everything will fall into place ~
'No Resistance, Allowing the Process to Happen'
More Translucent, More Conscious of the feeling body.
A different kind of Under*standing (Deist no more ego?)
Runs by Cosmic energy ~ Not a Global Conglomeration!
No more water crystals flowing through our Mother Earth ~
Three dimensional nano-reptiles breeding 744,000 Imprints.
Gave us the wrong < Dis*Illusional belief > Maya System.
Who's taking away our natural, timeless Spirits?
Look up, laying on the beach and read the sky.
Reflections of light, Stars and Planets orbiting
Micro*Cosmos * Macro*Cosmos
*

Coming down from a trip * there's No Turning back.
I didn't know I knew, so having less expectation ~
No blade of grass anywhere on Earth is the same.
All the freaks have freedom, realising we already have it!
With no movement~ there's no life. "Hey sexy Goddess ~
End of Illusory Stuff, going to the Limit, let the bubble Plop!
Mr. Micron you're built from a shiny Crystal hologram Inside.
Wrapped in holistic, mystical mystery or, 'Penis I like Venus!'
What Mind needs, mission on being a Satellite, inside Space.
Which part of him was Insane? And they're really Pure;
I mean Really poor! Let's share all the blessings here.
He must have seen something; Living in the moment.
Imaginary tomorrow is Now*Time the Ultimate teacher.
The Spirit of Light
The Spirit of Love
The Spirit of Truth
* Self-taught *
Super*natural

They're Not Free-range snails!
All I was left with was her shame and guilt at the bottom of the pit!
Fancy a cockroach cocktail, big dish of spiders or crabs?
"The coke was more important than me, our Love!"
Falling to pieces in a snow storm, left me to freeze.
"What does it mean?" Nothing!
Only Ego's Selfish-interest.
Heart, I think I felt a beat.
'It is what it is'
*

Is Real!
"Why don't we just bomb them all?
They can't kill us if they're all dead!"
Protecting humanity through mad inhumanity!
Black sites all over holy land, soaking in blood.
Bombing us all back into the dark ages righteously!
You were there too with your sadistic inquisition.
Insane, paranoia, Sociopaths running the Palace.
Who has the power making this diabolical tyranny?
Complete economic collapse by the financial cabal.
Instigated terrible, horrors of suffering and destruction!
*

Shebeen Patterns
My Sacred Heart, 'Give Peace a chance man!' Ego Freedom during Apartheid!
"A normal black guy has 3 wives, one his wife with 3 jobs and 6 kids, she keeps
the house while he gets money from the other two!" Must be some nice hovels..
"If a black dog fucks a white dog, the owner of the white dog can shoot the owner
of the black dog!" All got Kalashnikovs! Picked that fuckin' grape and squashed it!
A raging alcoholic coming out of his mother's womb, who came out of his mother's
womb a raging alcoholic, who came out of his mother's womb a raging alcoholic!
For all the cruel, inhumane oppression, exploitation of the blacks!
Can't kill that smile ~ Keeps it ALIVE!

Lollipop lady on Patrol
I wouldn't sign a Contract..
Everything will be ~ different
To hold on to something ~ Iconic
Is Bananas, is the grave, is the grace!
Just allow your*self to observe your feelings.
Allowance to ground that experience in reality.
There is so much Possession
It's dead - no life, gone.
Truth is in beingness
*

Primal Rose
Ourselves ~ Let it go
Not to have any involvement, be compassionate.
The need to be Loved ~ in a tender, feeling way
In one projection, can't show it ~
Being kept behind Locked doors!
Haven't seen that, for so long
She's holding back ~
"Can I trust this man?"
Be Open
but let it go, live freely,
never use buts, please;
buts ~ are all wrong.
By saying it, you are it.
'A Genius'
Proof is in the pudding.
Has the right to unfold ~
because you manifested it.
Everything is a Meditation
It's your relationship to the matter.
Smoking joints is a big Meditation so is dancing at Shiva Valley.
More direct, more to the source ~ always comes to frequencies.
"Allowing Space surrounding us, Not Separate ~ Consciousness"

Witness Original DNA.
Angry, Obsessive Mind, Selfish Mind, Jealous Mind, Ego, Possessive Mind…
Lustfully, enviously, greedy, Violent, sociopathic Mind; States of limited Mind.
Can be a Beautiful view in the Mind of a Conscious beholder of changing ~

*

Loosening it up in time & space now ~
Experiment in Synchronicity gives it Possibility
of Reflection, of multi*dimensional Personality.
"Pain is not a feeling ~ it is a Resistance
against the real sensations coming through"
You can relax with it & go with the experience.
Here you are Shiva, have the lot, let it happen.
Paying away your sins if you believe you have them.
A Confessional Box where money was more than Love.
"I'm happy that you called but what's on?"
Go for the feeling of what you are.
Natural seeds, cells worth more than Gold.
'The body to hold if you want to hold the body'
'Allowance to change or Resistance to the Pain'

*

An 'Unconventional' truth aroused the Happy & mellow ~
Coming out of music, reflections dissolving in rivers of grace.
Siddhartha the holy warrior of Compassion in the Middle
of the heart chakra, in the experience of the dhamma.
Frequency ~ Inorganic to organic trans-formation.
Shocking vibrations appearing real in the brain!
Now I can feel as deep as I want as I've been there ~
You want to feel free, tuning into the Rainbow ~ exactly!
Out in Nature, not holding back, getting the source code.
How to touch people with our auras in peace and harmony?
Use or misuse that Trust ~ Integrated Love load; explode!
Not 'Extreme interrogation' techniques, using psychologists
& disqualified medical workers for their key role in sustaining
prisoners' suffering! Is this the Global future we are allowing?

Revolutionary Heroine
Best not thinking what you say; judgmental.
"I go in fear, or I go in fear" or I go in Peace.
Electrical Orgasms * tension going up!
More ecstasy overflowing her well.
This Conscious Realisation.
(not a Jesus statue full of coke)
So Powerful, so dangerous, so worthy of going to Jail for!
I can give you the Best. Realised Feelings of lawful Rebellion.
Breaking into the Lingam Temple in a mini skirt & kinky boots.
Loving women with erotic intention; seductive, free expressions.
Do you want Slavery? Why?
*

Perihelion Masters
Our kids are Our hope for the future.
They have so much to tell us,
from their Unconditional Love
*

On the Cosmic Charasbang
The Conductor of a tram going to the Berlin Fusion festival.
'Welkomen' the direct approach going through that process.
Cleanse the body from the poisoning of our children.
It will happen by itself ~ No Information necessary.
The Best way by thought * Patterns that you throw.
Giving them all the Allowance to be ~
The mother's been dancing with Hari Krishna.
Her warm skin touching my arm.
Contacting a girl from the sweetest part of Venus,
engorging her clitoris ~ transmuting that frequency!
Came across Cosmic Inner Space in her sparkling eyes.
The only other thing he can put his energy into ~
More translucent not going into any fear quadrant.
"I believe I know." "What?"

Bliss Cookie
Lost 36 Levels Underground…
Have you found your (Elgin) Marbles?
Compulsive Obsession, a pensioned dictator,
never letting go of the TV. remote ~ Controller!
Dancing of the bubbles better on Acid.
Who has the best drugs, bondage boy?
We are All One energy over the Auric field.
Cosmic Revolution ~ If you react you're in it!
So many Angels around today * 46 +2 * Love chromosomes.
Stepping stones, Brain jumping with a new neuron transmitter.
A nice couple, two different Planets integrating one Milky Way ~
Gorgeous blonde Natalia, with sunglasses at two in the morning.
Through reflection you see yourself
We can enter Creation in any way.
Crossing with a Merkaba * it needs a strong Spark!
*

Ultra * Gravity
You can see the effects but not where it comes from.
Hun Sen where did Brother No 1 have his bunker?
They needed to get Mad, go visit death camp S-21!
Why can't people just relax and be Happy without genocide?
That's a good question; Nature knows how to take of it.
They're gonna get married in Heaven.
How good is that!
*

All that you want to see
"Oh, I lost my bindi tracker!"
Singing out of my heart
Rock & Roll devotion.
Surrendering to Love.
Feeling a Big Feeling
Liked her energy at once.

Fuck me Pink!
'An exclamation of surprise or wonderment'
Amazon's: 'Karma sutra' ~ Health, Family, Self Help guide.
'All definitions are approved by humans before publishing'
Psychological addiction - fitting the oil into the Cannabinoid receptors!
Walking around like Neo in a construct; say 'No' it's such a small word.
"Have I committed a crime officer or only broken the rule of law?"
Otherwise you've taken an oath to defend my natural rights.
He's only a witness not the judge, they have no jurisdiction!
"As God is my witness I was stopped unlawfully me Lud"
The case dismissed under Natural law, not making joinder.
It's the procedure, Corporate takeover by Commercial law.
Trampling all over your rights, our Queen will back you up!
"I have committed No Crime" Not usurping of your rights.
Your own jurisdiction, I am a King, "I am a LIVING MAN"
Fuck me gently!
*

Dense Heat Template
A High job sweeping the floor in the Buddha Hall.
The Intent ~ Tuning into the Glorious Mothership.
Orientation, manifesting her destiny, spinning stones.
'You had to have complete faith to walk off the Mountain'
"I saw a lot of white people with Nat King Cole records"
'One day a beautiful melody just started singing inside me'
The dreams of the 80's have now become reality.
The Whole Blue Print will collapse in on itself.
Realisation coming, the World will crumble.
Key the meaning, the understanding
*of the quantum flow of multi*dimensionality.*
New Earth from Mother Earth. Don't fuck her!
Let the Ozone hole heal, let the pollution out.
Icebergs melting water into the River Rhine,
Bluebell flowers blooming in mid December.

The High Notes
"Happy You Go Up for sure"
"Phone me if you want me"
Children give you so much love.
Be Strong, bliss of my life
Spheres reading between the lines ~
Don't have to win the lottery to win the Organic life.
Back to the freedom of Spirit, back to where you came from.
You don't know the feeling of.... Free of Charge.. get it?
*

"I ripped the shit out of her!"
Powers out there are all working against it, for themselves!
A Spiritual Planet (need to have disinterested Equilibrium)
Helping to change the Injustice with an 'Organic response'
'Where there is sweetness there are ants, the law of nature'
'Using your time against your will that's slavery, inhuman crime'
The Law is Not the Law it's only the Legal Society's system.
"You understand the charges?" "Yes" is 'Joinder!'
"You're fucked!" You are the Head of Your State.
The nature of the Beast; A Massive Deception!
"Are we having FUN yet?"
*

Totally Illegal
"Am I obliged to talk to you…
I do not want to talk to you…
Refuse to give your name…
Am I being detained or arrested?
I will not answer any questions.
I do not understand you…
I want a lawyer
I wish to remain silent!"
Thank You

Hunky Dory Street #136

She was laughing ~ Smiling all over her face.
Happy ~ All of them had that sort of quality.
"You gotta girl on your arm that you can
change anytime you want"
Your Cosmic ticket ~ the winning sperm.
"It was all effortless, 'Neti neti', boomsi in Phnom Penh"
200 ships turned up in Italy with 10,000 female slaves.
Sold them on the beach ~ "Quanto costa Bella?"
If it's for the highest good ~ it Manifests itself!
DNA. can't Reproduce the Cosmos in a test tube.
Surrender, It's Living now ~ natural trans*mutation.
Insane Karma's all gone, holding up light Vibrations.
No Separation, You're in Love or You're Not in Love.

*

You Are the Kaleidoscopic Sky

You go through the Matrix ~ of Creation to a new Matrix..
If you can activate Your brain, you're a Krishna reflection!
Transcendent tendency of the Plant Queen is to remind you
of how Amazingly, Incredibly beautiful, You are, we all are!
Connecting with the Higher self, to the self ~ of the One*self.
Intelligence, Knowledge, 'In Dream World' going to the Zone.
Starlight in the open Heart * of boundless, Love Unconditional.
Inter*dimensional realities, screaming Cosmic communication ~
Found written on a boomerang at an outback, Solar Light Center.
Put a wave of healing on Earth, welcome to the lilac crystal child.
Galaxies existing within You living outside apparent time barriers.
Ganesh Cybernetics-Transplanting an Elephant head to a human.
New Bio*Chip in the brain, OBEY-PAY; Are you feeling any Pain?
Your Mind is the Sky * thoughts coming & going in deepest Space
beyond any Astral Identity of light

*

Painting the Ashram Black

A new spin on it ~ your beautiful, undulating, crimson chakra.
Asks if it's right to be here, at this Great spot now? Of course!
'Cassandra Crossing' ~ going from one dimension to another.
When DNA. hits it explodes like a flower.
5th Black element * Cloning at Los Alamos.
Density got fucked up channeling life forces ~
They showed me how to read the hieroglyphics
A wave right to left ~ to the Underground Pyramid.
Connect and follow it to the source ~ Spirit & human.
"Having a right to be a bitch!" Pointless couldn't say NO!
Live snakes around her arms ~ turning into a dark crystal.
Wants to raise the vibration from a fucked up man in a suit.
From Dodgy City, covert enclaves of the Pirates ~ Free Will?
Presidents can't go to Area 51 or the Vatican's Mafia Temple!
It's all about the Divine, don't deceive, let's have it ~
Share it and Receive it ~ 'Whatever floats your boat.'
An Invitation, give it to me, so much love for humanity.
Just holding the energy, Healing the people with light.
Most are so closed down, they can't let go either ~
He started to channel to save the World, rubbed his feet.
"At least he's in his body." Two more minutes of red hot kisses,
he opened his eyes and fell in love with Artemis of the Wildland.
Ok You can take him to hospital for the fantastically deranged!
"I'll just shut up, listen and follow." Razzled, spangled, No Mind.
Psilocybin gateway opening to the stars, witnessing the Celestial.

*

Preyed Upon

"How do you say 'No' to God?" Almighty!
Words & Meanings & Actions-Reactions.
"As soon as he wrote, 'Imagine'
He had to fuckin' go!"

*

Choking Orca
"Money can't buy me love, can't buy me love…"
It's only make believe, manifesting the seeds ~
"They're only in it for the lust of money, plain and simple!"
The Biggest Killer in the sea, being greedy for plastic bags.
Confessions of a Milk man; "Like to get fanny in a frenzy!"
Bang against the wall! "I don't ever eat healthy"
"I can't just sit and empty my mind"
Birds know they're going to be eaten in a Battery Hen Pie!
*Giving ecosystem natural energy * is the frequency of Life.*

*

Flirting, Coquettish Angels
*More synchronous, Neocortex, Off * On ~ Changing.*
"An Elephant will carry you through the water."
Has the right to choose whatever he wants to do.
Becoming ~ to be, witnessing all that happens in the Mind.
Divine Fulfilment, Flower Power, feeling the Infinite Space ~
Gazing at beautiful Chekhovian women's light romantic eyes.
You want to do the best, I know.
It's nice ~ I smile

*

Jungley Love
Christ Consciousness
Crystal Consciousness
Being Conscious of your Consciousness
Don't think about it ~ You go through
*Witnessing never born * never gone*

*

Kali
I'm an Artist
& I need to see
Beauty

Darjeeling Dawn
"Do you miss me already?"
Practice makes Perfect, what?
Here comes another one…
Leave me in Peace ~ Finish.
It's happened now! Anticipation
"You are the gift already"
Let the moment run through you with No Resistance.
Escape the bad bubble gum of cocaine society!
*You are You * transparent density of the Trust.*
She was born at a sacred Peyote ceremony.
They tune you in with their funny kissing
Are you lying down ~ Strapped in?
*All around us * we recognise ourselves*
on the supreme nature mothership, flying through Space.
Surreal Jesus, consciousness coming on a shooting star.
You go through the Patterns to the Sacred flower of life
at the end
*

At this moment in time realise it's only a thought ~
*Going round a Psy*Vortex*Cortex behind my back!*
Feeling sad, betrayal, denial, rejection by someone you
really Loved and trusted through my sense of Ego-self.
My heart couldn't cope with another ounce of bullshit!
Neural Super-Highways into the pleasant New horizon.
What your mind thinks is important; watching it from afar ~
What's going on, happening inside your brain's just a delusion.
All these channels ~ can you remember one thing that was funny?
Replaced every shitty thought with blissful ones, a Labial workout!
What thought do you want inside your head before you croak?
"I'd love this girl but I wouldn't be in love with her"
Did I cure myself of the emotional attachment?
N E W   F E E L I N G S   of   B E I N G   H A P P Y

You & Me In Sputnik Relativity
Has seen the Planet, why the lie?
"Don't take it too seriously"
With Love you can kiss a frog ~
turning into an Aztec Prince with Quetzal feathers.
Allowing themselves to receive hot Russian chicks!
Are we on a Mission just to have Fun? "Da, Spatzeba"
Singing Sonatas from the heart of streaming sunbeams.
"But I won't sleep with you if you've got fleas"
Who do I think I am to disagree?
As you do ~ 100%, a real devotee really flipped out!
No she's gone into another enlightening experience.
Went into a black hole of Hell and came back again.
Feeding his cows mangoes in monsoon's lush, falling rain.
Full green nature ~ lots of growth
*

Dancing with light
They picked the fruit of duality * Universal Moons * Suns.
Kicked out of Paradise for biting a naked Love apple ~
Didn't need the knowledge to be in Y/our natural state.
Not having the right to stay but can always Celebrate!
Cause affecting the Ascension of Masters.
'This Temple Is You'
*

Empty Your Temple
It's the musical notes telling you that you're here.
It's all Zen, in What I Imagine to be Real ~ Globally.
The Power of Fear ~ Run by a Texas Oil Corporation
The Planet Will survive, not looking good for us tho' .....
The most common Alien face; cows in the middle of a road.
Out of duality into real relativity ~ "Who am 'I' to disagree?"
You see You only; I see Me only, without Us ~ being lonely.
All about My Mind interpreting and Reacting to the World ~
Awareness Acting on a stage of Conditioning and Projection.

Spinning Mosaics
A Big Satanic Temple.
Attached to a nipple clamp
Karma in cellular pictures
Trust in the Trusting
Manipulation ~ not hidden
Something in the spinning molecules
Sitting there like a rabbit in the headlights!
Waiting ~ Put out a green light.
Why kill the mosquito
when your window's always open?
Close the timeless door on dualities.
Psychedelic Venus riding her Tiger of delusion
*

Hindu Surrealism
Saw all the colours exploding in the cortex of his brain.
Nicely done in a virtual turquoise, sea aquarium.
It's Inside projecting Outside with no treatment
*now you are One * in the Galactic tropical jungle ~*
Building a force of creation, 'Brahmanda' Cosmic egg
travelling in all the lands ~ without lies of separation
being in the centre point of the Universal perspective.
*Choosing Freedom of Mind-sets into multi*dimensions.*
Observing the program of a Pleiadian pin-up calendar.
*

Could be Funky Creators, what do you want?
Our enemies are our own best friends; Oh really!
Need the Relativity ~ Processing duality experience.
Opening the eyes ~ to the freshness of Spring.
Changing seasons, doing her magic trip now
In One as One ~ timelessness of Space.
*Living as it is * One with existence*
You are in it ~ no longer resistance to it.
Falls in oneness "got it" just a reflection

Yakshi in St.Theresa
Prana fruit * You see that you are forever ~
'Heart the Key of the Lock to the Cosmos'
Who are they? "Just egoists fuckin' between lines of coke"
"I am just Observing" the girl from Ipanema with a Caprinha.
A deal too good to be true, white coke whores from the hills!
"Why would you want to say No?" Sweet honey child ~
with peppermint eye drops; looking for the Perfect consort.
Got to give it all away to be fully tuned ~
You go in ~ no distractions, sweating in Alta Paraiso
with Ayuhuasca rhythms building up the Sacred Spirit.
Allowance, Oming through the 4ᵗʰcrystallized chakra.
Co*Creative in the heat of Vibrations, synchronous city.
Good to truly satisfy the body * Mind and Cosmic Spirit.
Relax go into the Unconditional love of a beating heart
*
Rebirthing Cosmic Gompa
Intention of the first 6 breaths
Cleansing the chimney ~
Sunset changes your Mind
Existence is running * making the body easier.
No resistance, dissolving ~
gleaming through your eyes
*
Progressing Death's Processing
A pressure we experience in the 3ʳᵈ dimension
becoming * a crystal shining in the Universe ~
Restructuring light going throughout the body.
Growing stocks of Titanium in the garden
*
Stupa fried Archaeologist rooting a Paleontologist
Specialised in Flea Markets especially in Amsterdam.
Finding a Big Brother Reality TV show, Full Brain/less
Washing Programming, cycle, spin, dried out like a pea.

"No Way I'll Stop"
"They let her smoke charas in the Police Station!"
"Love gives you energy ~ it continually moves"
"I've been out with your mates Molly & Mandy"
Creating in Trance, breaking patterns up
Make your own melody
Pop*Trance in Fantasy Land.
'Puff the Magic Dragon'
getting stoked, simple zone.
Long term stoner ~ don't do very much.
Spending the Monsoon with the girl you Love
who is gorgeous
*

Stupendo Lounge

Learning how to do nothing is hard, watching grass grow.
All got to do with witnessing the Mind ~ processing of duality.
Because it's all Oneness ~ each cell connected to the Earth!
Plans, don't have any let's see what happens to the butterfly.
Don't have to do anything*Lilies aware in the field and pond.
They're shanti people, so much more quietness in their Mind.
Feelings of relative conditionings ~ We know what we know,
we don't know what we don't know, just mental-movement.
It's Ego-Mind playing games ~ watching it evolve inside.
Travelling along tangents ~ patterns going back awhile.
Tuning in to happy smiles; we are equal, Living People.
Being here don't have to be in any 'Social system'
Enjoy your free time ~ or become incarcerated?
Beautiful hearts, what happens always changes.
That's why we're here for self-realisation.
*

Pre-Conception

'Time' for a Shrink ~ Hitting Skid Row
Taught me 'Non-Involvement'
Wonderfully * Random

The Psychic Wife
You pay for it right at the Time and move on
If it was emotional it would be Love
again & again spiraling out in bliss ~

*

Defining However Much
Imagining outside your self
In control of yourself ~ Who is?
Grateful not to be ~ a 'Victim'
In this Mental-ego force field
Spinning out in Chaos ~
embracing it ~ from Inside You.
Focusing on depth ~ fewer distractions.
*Channeling * Cosmic meadows * Tuning In.*
Is this the hardest Meditation in the World?
Animals at play, celebrating their own nature
In the middle of the jungle
Singing to a bird.

*

Eight minutes to get to Earth from 100 million miles away
Inflation, austerity ~ going to work on a hard boiled Ego.
Over flying the Stock market in his own super-drone!
"At least you can realise we're all living in a full illusion"
*Official: 'A One Mile Weather Balloon' * Open the UFO files!*
They finally made themselves Visible, landing in west Texas.
St Germain ascending in a Spaceship, liberate Your feelings.
Free people from debt, economic crash arriving on the next wave.
Meanwhile 1000 flying saucers are parked up in front of MIR.
Signs of Intelligence, "You Can't Win" we didn't realise it yet!
Trying to tell us something ~ "We're all Cosmic beings."
*Transmuting In a human body * our Realistic Space-suit.*
Energy released of a billion Atomic bombs in seconds
can fit into you a million times!
The heartbeats of the Sun

In Ages
"Just got mugged in Calangute again!"
Mine was full of bananas and a bag of weed.
Who hasn't swallowed the Pill? Who can we Trust?
Not the Police, the Panchayat, or Ministers at the top,
Priests are in League and not even the local Coroner!
Cosmic Nonsense (so don't get caught up in fame & glory).
How powerful is Addiction ~ 'Shit happens, Magic happens'
Magic Mushrooms growing in cow dung on Maui happen too

*

The Box
'Trying to Achieve so much ~
when we Already got Everything'
'Raison d'etre' ~ Energetic being being,
letting it just happen, 'Wu wei' ~ Effortless effort.
The Trap, all these Ideas, are in our Egoic-head!
Losing our energy, distracted, where's it gone Baba?
All just One, witness the Illusion of Mind and the next.
Stop judging Your Self ~ be a free spirit
That's how easy it is, creating the same phase.
Just being, not doing
"The day I got there the rains started"

*

Starry Eyed Discovery
Same vibration as children
with their frequencies
Let them Exercise.
Don't Think, come ~
Nature in the centre
Falling in full Oneness.
Waiting for young Stella lighting up, shining her own fire burst.
Every atom all around us was made from the heart of a Star ~
Creating shining Stars on Earth, you have the gift of free will ~
"Helped to liberate Belsen, knew what people were capable of!"

Isolation Tank
"I'm just happy in a swimming pool"
Weightlessness ~ losing connection.
Duality is integral to the movement...
The Mind is an Alien ~ Ego construct.
They're coming from somewhere.
Out of the Greater Mind Ocean
They're not smiling anymore ~ sour faces.
You wanna be where everyone's smiling.
'I know where I am!'
"I'm here now
I'm not there and then...."

*

Realisation Treatment
He's Not the Laughing Buddha
He's a Happy Gorilla with Empathetic Reality.
Looking deeply into the streaming river Flux ~
Seeing a big banana enjoying carnal pleasures,
falling into the fires of conscious, multi-Orgasms.
Wanting to go out of my impermanent mind and body
makes complete Sense, celebrating beyond beyond.
"In the morning everything was fine, birds were singing.
Superwoman giving me a Cosmic, lingam massage!

*

'You're already it'
Not the drugs ~ going for yourself.
Allowing to Love Yourself ~ Super Sensitivity.
Make Puja to your Sacred being.
Divine is Indescribable darshan
to me not an accessory but necessary.
Don't decorate the Temple with your own soul.
Head to foot black Hijabs with 500 pairs of designer shoes!
Opening the doors to Heaven ~ Pinch me

*Aliens in Sao Paulo * 4th largest city in the World*
"Take me to your dealer" ... I love it, obrigado!
Put it on a Poster for "A Million Rials ~
Get Kate Moss here quick!" 'Guapa'
You'll become richer or poorer ~ separating, dualism.
Can't compare anything to Acid or Magic mushrooms!
Witnessing the Cosmic unfolding ~ of a Lotus flower

*

They raped her with a brolly printed with a Union Jack.
Mystery goes on; Harmonic chords in tune with the Moon.
Have to leave the dimension of the Mind, Greed, Ego, Pride.
Transcends the Brilliance of a Super computer & infinitely more.
My Mind has to go with it ~ birthed into a Sub-Conscious realm.
"Did You Know that humans evolve synergetically?"

*

'Enlightenment'
It's just another word-Formation, like 'Materialisation'
Wisdom of Enlightenment is seeing closer to death!
'I AM WHAT I AM' nothing more egotistical than that!
You know even if you don't know ~ it's always changing.
But being Conscious of it so not taking things personally!

*

Clear Waves
The Mind helps the Mind dictate.
Just techniques to wash away
the attachments and fears ~
Bigger Brain In Love

*

Like they know the tree
Isolation, Alienation, Polarisation, steps ~ in a Police State.
Where's the Good olde Magick! Seeing feudal places as Dead.
Agonising over the lesser of two evils. Choose happy & Peace.
It's Living ~ You wouldn't get the Separation.
Artistic expressions fulfilling all our senses ~

Bumpy Sticker

A Tyrannical State suspended Habeas Corpus; our 'Natural Law' what's that?
'The Home of Extraordinary Rendition' - 'Water Boarding' Sports -TORTURE!
Something to be Proud of; put it in your unholy Constitution, written in blood!
Who's exploiting above all the resources of an undemocratic Full Congress?
Economic Warfare, halted the growth of poor, sovereign Cuba.
Tried stopping Fidelity, dancing Salsa in the streets of Havana.
Magicians at a Sun Eclipse climbing to the apex of a Pyramid.
Great meeting 300 mike Teddy Bears riding round on bicycles.

*

Fluffy Muscled Teletubbies

"She's always been a wet velvet pussy" coming for a caress.
"I believe in Happiness" ~ Giving and Receiving generously.
Repeating…. Existence is running through You ~ always.
Not your Ego running it if You choose, contacting with life.
It's so simple ~ letting go of all Ingrained, conditional ties.
Existence running through her telling her what to do or not.
You have to go through it to see, transcend ego's Identities.
How to dissolve it ~ even with every fear & horror ~ 'As it is'.
Arthritis really showing you to tune into the aches and pains.
Feeling Sensations in your Mind being sub-conscious' flow ~
deep into the sub-atomic, into the cellular, your blood stream.
Taking you to your DNA's origins in multi-holistic Universes.
Being with our true essence ~ fulfilling our divine destiny

*

Fake Media & Puppetry

Not so strange here; 'If you don't pay your car tax, we'll crush you Car!'
Illegal in Natural Law, not committed a crime, they have no Jurisdiction.
Built a Central School for 'Black Psychological Operations' - On Whom?
On You, on all of us mate. Coercion ~ in Bedfordshire, UK. of all places!
Where's the human consciousness of those responsible in Government?
Divine energy in every atom ~ Cosmic Conqueror of all the galaxies.
Slapped him all the way to the door, psychopath, invader, marauder.
At twilight!

Strategies of a pair of lungs
Don't have to practice breathing ~
Already Is * synchronicity Alive.
Combining life with life itself.
Cherries are Pain Killers…
Loving to do it from an open Heart
No Thinking, Ego or My Politics!
Don't set any goals for the future
to Fuck your Unconscious Mind.
To show who is in Control!
Find Yourself in Peace ~
then you're allowed to die.

*

Obstacles of Mind
"When you're gone you're gone" - Kaput!
700 German new tax laws to fuck your kopf!
New Age Ashram cleaning the nano-cell mirrors;
energy coming through the meeting; what is real?
Only over your Crystal can you reflect anything true.
Moving into a Conscious Bio-Energetic spectrums.
Give it a Spiritual note for the Inspiration

*

I'm cancellin' me Party!
Fed up with all these DJ's ego ~
Thinking about a house, just do it.
Nothing more to do with the Outside.
You've had that experience now Inside.
So you don't give it yourself anymore ~
Everything that is a con, more distractions.
A bigger Deception, the Devil in the Devil in
the Devil in the Devil in the Devil ~ changing.
You go out of your Mind into essential Space.
When You sense it, when you really feel it…

Trying to Control Intel
'Language of Light'
The Good News Is * being the moment.
We've discovered 100 million galaxies out there!
'The Chinese Circus erecting its tent in Rockefeller Centre'
Focus of the Intention, Centred Concentration ~ reflection.
Rays of Shiva spirals colliding with whirring Insane Branes.
Human Nature
Can't do it if you don't let them ~
Increased Control verses the Coming Breakthrough
*

New-Age Projection
* All sub-atomic cellular karmic mirrors *
The energy comes through ~ the contacting.
"Take the disciples away, the 'true believers'
and you've just got one bloke on his own!"
Only over the crystal * Can you reflect anything.
As a still, calm lake will give a clear reflection, so the quietened mind.
(Socialism/Capitalism/NWO other ISMs want to Stop people's freedom)
Spiritual vibration ~ not Conglomerate's domination, exploitation…
for true Inspiration
*

'When You Are Gone ~ You Are Gone.' Gone…
Designed Innumerable laws to Fuck y/our Mind.
Taoism gently shows You Who's Not in Control ~
Labour government's 3000+ new laws in 10 years!
Find Yourself in Peace with nature
then you're allowed to die.
*

Cerise * Palette
Psychoactive Palaces ~
Lots of Purples & Oranges
All moving

<u>The Rainbow way</u>
Fun For Everyone
So Precious
We don't have to look for it ~
"It's already here * Inside us all"
Surrender ~ to Unconditional Love.
Creation in Space beyond the mind.
Material will come!
Omnipresently
*

<u>A Collection of Cosmic Keys</u>
Pain is a resistance to not letting the feeling go
Aluminium Strip Lights giving us all brain disease ~
Low energy - Lighting systems being detected…
Without the heat, fluffy no thorns, trapped in our bodies.
Our natural Speed ~ don't wear brogues found in a bog.
All the energy goes to Earth holding on or not, Surrender.
Rubber tyres still holding the life force of the plant planet.
Whole energies from the 1st Mescaline juice in Psyche *
Tropical, San Pedro, Lima ~ let the sensations flow again.
"Put the cactus in the Peyote blender"
Supplying them fresh
*

<u>Releasing Synergy</u>
Who wants to go to the 'Decadence Shopping Festival'?
And Who wants to go to the Next Level ~
When you are in Tune everything comes.
Singing Tones having the right frequency
found the perfect harmony in a vibrating throat chakra.
Connection to Emotion * realises the Idea * in the Heart.
What was the Intent? How to be a Cosmic bodhisattva,
singing spiritual mantras in a dynamic, natural Universe.
Don't be cynical, building Resonating, Toning Pyramids.
Already given to us ~ flying all the time in the here * now

Spent the Ideals
to get the business….
Mr. & Mrs. Crocodile been here a long time ~
All these birds descended from the Dinosaurs.
"You dropped the best, clean bit!"
In a room with 1000 mosquitoes!
London has its place in the Cosmos.
It's alive and flowing ~ cause & effect.
Fearful not to have enough money!
"You wasted so much Energy"

*

On Your Wavelength
"You don't have to drink to Party"
Pranayam Ayuhuasca on 'Santo Daime Day'
An Original Life
Heavy drumming, Chill out, No more Clinging Please.
"There's a surfeit of hungry pussy in the irradiated sea"
Truly ~ There are humble people.

*

Many Names for a 'Ticket to Ride'
Dossier found in a town on Mercury ~ throwing the Runes.
*Invocation through pendulums * dancing Antigravity fields.*
*Intuition makes Zen*Sense all part of me ~ Self-realisation.*
Put it on the Internet for Free, of course, fully Censored brain.
Accepting it all graciously.
The Right Recipe (Global warming as it is; consciously!)
Distorted by ET Aliens, wanting to live in CO2 awareness!
Is it only Greed, we've been taken over by 'Absolute Power!'
Where's humanity, all true it's only how you resonate with it ~
Actions of Devotion made over a Lifetime; devotion to Vishnu,
even simple gifts, offerings of berries from an Untouchable Dalit.
Free to fly ~ given a pass through to the 4th dimension!
A guru says, "My dear Sir, you're quite mistaken about yourself,
You are not the person you take yourself to be."

Transitory Undercurrents

The end of FORM ~ 'Nothing' is just another word.
Science says, 'energy has no beginning & no end'
I saw at once they had their Attention on Reiki....
Then I blew them away ~ "How good you are to me!"
What it's like in the timeless * dimension * be aware, there
is no time, always changing so nothing exists even your self ~
Identity is a fleeting mirage ~ don't become attached to any of it!
The journey's been rebooted through a dopamine tunnel, we can
break in all sorts of directions, don't take it personally, Me, mine, I;
only your Ego's demands; realising this change in the light ~ now.
Multi*dimensional FORMS transmuting golden, conscious Alchemy.
Omniscient, omnipresent even in a weak body y/our spiritual destiny.
Eros & a shining Tantric Goddess, sensations of our fractal*hologram.
It's where life comes from ~ Raw Honey Yoni * Jnana marga Creation.
Interpretations of another Big Bang, splish, splash, plip-plop!
Humans are unlike animals ~ They're all naturally programmed!
Enchanting your lapsang cup of tea by chanting an Om mantra.

*

Ecstatic * Dancing

Stepping In * Stepping Out
Stepping stones... No Go Zones!
Where time stands still ~ in present infinity.
LSD & PSY*trance; no past memory or future imagination!
What I was thinking, absent mindedly, being in the here and now.
Highest absorption being One ° with the Divine.

*

Cosmological Eye

Your mother gave birth, gave you life ~ what to do with this gift?
Without her you wouldn't exist to become self-aware.
'Who am I, where do I come from, where am I going?'
Discipline from out of Love ~ it's always changing.
No attachment to the mind is Tantra * Satsang.

<u>Breaking out of a Shell</u>
NOW-Global Empire serving Satan's Babylon Babble!
Lord God Nimrod cruising through the Milky Way ~
After the flood ~ Separated them with different tongues.
The key to Acid
Being Open* beyond your mind.
Embracing ~ the Universe
*

Pagan1
Star * Fire
*

<u>Sufi Whirled</u>
Rumi left Religion
for a relationship ~
with the truly Divine.
Walking within light
*

<u>AC. Gravitation</u>
The Earth only exists
for sense gratification of your body*mind!
Awareness ~ enjoying all Its distractions.
Sex the same High * pleasure refractions.
All to do with such Vibrational ~ frequencies
Observing the Planet of Maya as detached.
Your 3rd eye * Witnessing of No-Mind-Object.
When you were mentally-FORMED as a thought.
Go beyond mind's limits it can't exist, only is space.
Rising in flames to the energetic Heavenly realms.
That Magic Touch, her magic, compassionate touching.
Golden Bindoo rays shining on a Burmese beauty Queen.
The Junta put her under House Arrest for being an Avatar!
Meditating in silent Space realizing mental dreaming
for a Peaceful *Resolution * R*evolution.
Miracle after Miracle after Miracle ~

The Top Devotion
Interface with the Best ~ What do you do with it?
Go Mad with it, Enjoy It ~ eating Lotus petals.
It's beautiful and very Precious
What to do? Love it
*

Count Your Blessings
Perfect Populating, leaves of a tree....
Innocence of reactions ~ Delight*fullness.
Wild Cherry root, Indian ginseng, turmeric,
Three Doshas, free Ayur*Vedic fruit concentration.
Free-falling on snakeroot with a ferocious black panther.
'A King came with lots of slave girls from around the Planet.'
He got 15 years for bringing 2 kg. of raw chocolate into Goa!
Sky dancer with 1 kg. of MDMA in NYC; What's happenin?
When it's taken away then you realise what a blessing it is.
To walk & breathe properly ~ Prana dancing in your nerves.
There's nothing to believe, just sit, quietly observe the senses.
It's All Mind stuff happening, distractions enslaving us to it.
Get your head around that ~ "I come here to transcend!"
You either know or you don't know or neither or all ~
*

Energetic Vedas
She that injected Shaktivari ~
can handle too many husbands!
The real genetic code in your infected shit.
She was a nice girl you know what I mean?
We're gonna sort the world out, who else is gonna do it?
Nobody I know.
*

A Coke head
'He Spanked the High Life ~
"I'm hanging out with a load of Crazies!"
Let the river lead you to the Ocean ~

Precepts: You're not there; perspectives & proportions ~
Unfolding of 1000 petalled * Potentials & supra-perceptions.
Direct Creation, walk to Muktinath, on a Summer's afternoon.
A beautiful World, communication amidst the Himalaya peaks.
Crystal Consciousness >:< the Mind our Inner net,
thinking, feeling, believing, breathing, going further
Allowing & Receiving ~ next steps, stepping.
Informed thing always in the detail, wording,
bothers your soul, keep super flexible ~
We are coming through Cosmic code...
*

"I feel like going out and breaking 100 hearts!"
Each line Inspires me ~ Aware of Streams of Consciousness.
Creative expressions, "Yesterday I did some Psycho*actives"
You pay for it right at the Time and move on ~
If it was emotional it would be true Love.
Spiraling in unconditioned blissfulness
*

Spinning at the speed of light ~ translucent Merkabite.
Shortcut to Heaven on a golden ball.
Fast Track body channeling ethereal.
'Consciousness not Information ~
Everything Is in the Allowance
*

Happy
Enlightenment ~ can wait
*

Lao Tsu's Creativity
'The more you know ~
the less you understand'
It's the now ~
It's always been about the now
And it's Wild!

ABOUT SUNNY JETSUN

*Inspired by the sixties Sunny started traveling the world in 1970.
His spiritual journey on the hippie trail to India took him through ~
San Francisco, Los Angeles, London, Amsterdam, Paris, Vancouver,
Sidney and Kathmandu to Varanasi. His arrival on the sub-continent
was the beginning of writing autobiographical verses capturing his travel
experiences, encounters with remarkable people and his quest for self-
realization. Combining experimentation with drugs, sex, rock & roll, art,
meditation, Love and life in general. Sunny started to open up to a multi-
dimensional Universe. He lived the mantra, "Turn on, tune in, drop out"
realising Mind's-illusions, inspired by deeper feelings of holistic nature,
empathy* energy * Space.*

*Over four decades Sunny has written and published 28 books of poetry,
created over one hundred paintings, travelled the World and considers
his masterpiece to be his daughter. He has spent the past fifteen years
in Goa, India, inspired by the freedom to experience and idealism of
human consciousness.*

Sunny Jetsun books and art are available on the web at:

*Website: www.sunnyjetsun.com
Facebook: www.facebook.com/sunnyjetsun
Amazon: www.amazon.com/author/sunnyjetsun
Smashwords: www.smashwords.com/profile/view/sunnyjetsun*

www.ingramcontent.com/pod-product-compliance
Lightning Source LLC
Chambersburg PA
CBHW020509030426
42337CB00011B/298